how to solve word puzzles

Philip Carter and Ken Russell

D&B PUBLISHING

www.dandbpublishing.com

First published in 2005 by D&B Publishing,
PO Box 18, Hassocks, West Sussex BN6 9WR.

British Library Cataloguing-in-Publication Data
A catalogue record for this book is avalable from the British Library.

ISBN 1-904468-19-5

All sales enquiries should be directed to:
D&B Publishing, PO Box 18, Hassocks, West Sussex BN6 9WR, UK
Tel: 01273 834680, Fax: 01273 831629
e-mail: info@dandbpublishing.com
www.dandbpublishing.com

Cover Design by Horatio Monteverde.
Layout, typesetting and graphics by Mora Monteverde
Production by Navigator Guides.
Printed and bound in Finland by WS Bookwell.

Contents

Introduction

The English language, the most commonly spoken language in the world, has evolved from an awkward native dialect, the tongues of various invaders and the importation of other foreign words.

The basic element of the English language is Teutonic, or German, and the dialects of the various English and Saxon tribes which overran England during the fifth to seventh centuries belonged to the West Germanic group of the Indo-Germanic family of languages. To a basis of Anglo-Saxon words the Norman conquest added many Norman -French words of Latin origin to which were added many more words from Latin during the Renaissance. Finally, with the expansion of the British Empire, words were introduced from countries such as India, and other terms introduced by sailors and travellers from all parts of the world.

The result is a language consisting of some half a million words and spoken by an estimated 400 million people throughout the world. Because of the way it has evolved, the English language is rich in alternative words, such as *work* and *labour*, *friendly* and *amicable*, and is one of the most expressive of all tongues.

The English language is, to us, a bottomless treasure chest of delight. We take great pleasure in creating chaos from it, for that is what a puzzle compiler is - a creator of chaos, and, having thrown out the challenge, we hope that you derive an equal amount of pleasure from sorting out the chaos and restoring order

Playing with words is a universal activity. Word puzzles are probably the most popular and widely published of all puzzles. We all have to understand and speak the language to communicate, and the challenge of solving a word puzzle is one to which most of us like to respond.

This book attempts to remove the mystique from some of the more popular type of word puzzle by explaining their history, how some such puzzles are constructed, together with hints to enable you to become more proficient at solving them.

By far the best way to learn how to solve word puzzles, however, is by constantly practising on them. Our aim in this book is first and foremost to entertain you, and at the same time present you with the opportunity for practise on the various different types of word puzzle that you are likely to encounter, and at the same time strengthen your powers of vocabulary.

For those who are not already word puzzle addicts we hope that as a result of reading this book you will become a convert to the world of cryptic clues, word squares, cryptograms, palindromes, word searches, acrostics and homonyms, but above all we hope that this puzzle compilation brings you many hours of pleasure.

 I - Warm Ups

Introduction:

Variety being the spice of life, our first section consists of twenty-five different types of word puzzle all designed to limber up your mind for what is to follow.

1. Verbosity

In an endeavour to occasion an impediment that may lead to difficulty I am tossing an instrument used for securing small metal blocks, causing it to alight within the confines of mechanism in progress.

What am I doing?

2. Find A Phrase

Find the starting point and work clockwise to spell out a phrase (3, 2, 11 - letters long). Only alternate letters have been shown, and you have to provide the missing letters.

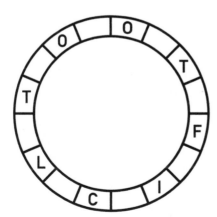

Complete the names of the eight animals (only alternate letters have been shown). Then rearrange the first letters of each of the animals to find a ninth animal.

* E * N * E * R

* Y * L *

* P * S * U *

* O * I * L *

* O * L *

* N * G * R

* N * E * O * E

* R * A * I * L *

4. Letter Change

In each of the following change one letter only from each word to produce a well-known phrase, for example chose ball = close call

add ode cut

Carl tie tone

on deer later

otter dish so cry

I kiss in US food am I milk

of tie toil

put any cried

keen in ewe put

lad town tie lad

mass she back

5. Saying In Bits

A phrase, which it is advised you should never do, has been sliced up into 3-letter bits and the bits then rearranged in alphabetical order. Can you reconstruct the saying?

For example: find the quote would be split into fin/d th/e qu/ote and the bits rearranged into alphabetical order thus: dth, equ, fin, ote

emo, hor, ift, kag, loo, nth, sei, uth

6. Add A Letter

Add one letter, not necessarily the same letter, to each word, at the beginning, middle or end, to find seven words that all have something in common.

how, rat, loop, big, put, bare, cane

7. Geezer's Teasers

The answer to each clue is a rhyming pair of words, for example, unhappy young man = sad lad

frighten a Prime minister

without support

grey matter depletion

South American mammal's histrionics

an extended step

elite squad

flip quickly through scheme

grasp lash

restrict lovemaking

more crafty member
of a religious order

8. Two Sayings

Start at one of the stars and finish at the other and work from letter to adjacent letter horizontally and vertically, but not diagonally, to spell out a well-known proverb. Every letter is used, once each only.

```
            *
A    M    T    R    O
N    O    O    B    T
Y    S    S    E    H  *
C    K    P    H    T
O    O    O    I    L
```

When you have solved the above puzzle try to find another proverb (4, 5, 4, 5, 4) which means exactly the opposite of the one above, by solving the anagram:

mark my shaking hand-towel

9. Find The Word

What word goes in front of all these words to make new words?

	ward
	shield
****	**pipe**
	lass
	age
	burn

10. Missing Link

Find a 3 - letter word that completes all three words on the left-hand side, and prefixes all three words on the right-hand side.

am		anger
leg	***	ear
up		long

11. X Y Z

Solve the clues to find four six-letter words. The same three letters are represented by XYZ in each word.

XYZ***   member of the legal profession

*XYZ**   scratched with nail

**XYZ*   African country

***XYZ   lawbreaker

12. Code Word

MINERAL   (ENIGMA)   KINGDOM

Using the same rules as in the example above, what word should appear in the brackets below?

ASTAIRE   (* * * * * *)   TINWARE

Insert two letters in each set of brackets so that they complete the word on the left and start the word on the right. The letters inserted, when read downwards in pairs, should spell out an 8 - letter word.

TA (* *) RT

SI (* *) SK

MO (* *) AR

ME (* *) LY

14. Three – Letter Words

Insert a girl's name into the bottom line to complete nine 3 - letter words reading downwards.

H	S	N	F	O	T	S	R	C
U	E	O	O	W	O	K	A	U
*	*	*	*	*	*	*	*	*

15. Find A Word

What word is indicated by the clues below?

second ballot

centre of Chicago

sixth former

first offender

non-starter

satisfactory conclusion

bottom end

16. Tiles

Rearrange the tiles so that every two adjacent letters form a word, and two related words can be read around the outer edge.

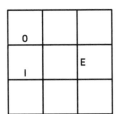

17. No Vowels

A well-known phrase has had all its vowels removed and has been split into groups of three letters. What is the phrase?

All remaining letters are in the same order.

FRB   TTR   RFR   WRS

18. Palindromes

The word Palindrome is derived from a Greek word *palindomos*, meaning *running back again*. A palindrome is a word, or phrase, or even longer literary work, which reads the same backwards as forwards. Examples of palindromic words are *madam, radar* or *level*, and examples of phrases are: *God a dog, madam I'm Adam, draw o coward, sad I'm Midas, sex at noon taxes*, and even *sex at my gym taxes* !

Many longer examples have also been compiled, for example *Tell a plateman on a morose damside by me to note my bed is made so Roman on a metal pallet*.

A.

Now complete the ten palindromes below by inserting the missing word/s:

Niagara, O **** again

Dennis and **** sinned

Now Ned I am a ****** nun, Ned I am a maiden won

Snug & raw was I ere * *** war & guns

Sums are not set as a test on *******

Nurse, I spy *******, run

Sir, I demand, I am a **** named Iris

Kay, a red nude ****** under a yak

Doc, note, I dissent, a fast never prevents a *******, I diet on cod.

'Tis **** on a visit

B.

Now insert the letters:

AAAAACDGIINOOP

into the following once only to complete the palindrome:

* **G ! A **N** ** * P***D*

19. Pangram

A pangram is a sentence that contains every letter of the alphabet, for example, the typists' test sentence *The quick brown fox jumps over the lazy dog.*

Complete the sentence below with the missing consonants so that it contains every one of the 26 letters of the alphabet at least once.

E *I*E *O*I *I*A*** *U** *UI****

20. Complete The Crossword

What word should complete the crossword below?

In each of the following start at one of the corner squares and spiral clockwise around the perimeter, finishing at the centre square, to spell out the 9 - letter words. You must provide the missing letters.

22. Non-Stop

Place the letters in the grid to produce two related words with the aid of the clue

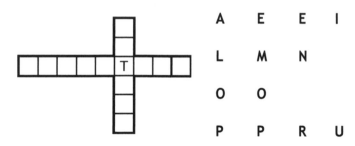

A	E	E	I
L	M	N	
O	O		
P	P	R	U

Clue : non-stop

23. Antonyms

Add one letter, not necessarily the same letter, to each pair of words in the front, middle or end, to find two words that are opposite in meaning

hop	dead
boar	lad
solid	right
reel	raw
beak	coy

24. Conversions

A.

Make ICE into SKATER by following these instructions and producing good English words at each stage.

		ICE
i.	change a letter	***
ii.	change a letter	***
iii.	add three letters	SKATER

B.

Put ROD into PISTON by following these instructions and producing good English words at each stage.

		ROD
		ROD
i.	change a letter	***
ii.	change a letter	***
iii	change a letter	***
iv	add three letters	PISTON

25. Word Circle

Complete the four 6 - letter words so that the same two letters that finish the first word start the second word, the same two letters that finish the second start the third, the same two letters that finish the third start the fourth, and the same two letters that finish the fourth are the same two letters that start the first word, to complete the circle.

* * C U * *

* * B U * *

* * N N * *

* * A P * *

II - Anagrams

Introduction:

An anagram is any of several word puzzles based upon the rearranging of letters in words. There are many variations on the basic theme several of which are used in psychological testing, the most common being the single solution anagram in which a set of scrambled letters are given and the testee is required to find the word they spell out, for example, the letters MOCURTPE can be rearranged to spell out the word COMPUTER.

Anagrams are also frequently used in crossword puzzles as part of a cryptic clue and we will explore their use in this context in greater depth later in this book.

The origin of anagrams is ascribed to a Greek poet, Lycophron. He lived during the fourth century BC and was brought to Egypt by King Ptolomy where he amused the king's court by inventing flattering anagrams of their names. Originally an anagram was simply a word which, when reversed, formed another word, for example TIME/EMIT, STRESSED/DESSERTS. The word anagram is derived from Greek; *ana* meaning *backwards* and *gramma* meaning *a letter*.

The best anagrams are those where the rearranged letters bear some relationship to the original word or name, for example, the letters of the word SOFTHEARTEDNESS can be rearranged to form the phrase OFTEN SHEDS TEARS and the word DORMITORY can be anagrammed into the phrase DIRTY ROOM.

Equally entertaining are antigrams, which are anagrams where the letters of a word are rearranged to form a word or phrase meaning the opposite. Examples of this form of word play are INFECTION (fine tonic), ENORMITY (more tiny) and PROTECTIONISM (nice to imports).

The ability to solve anagrams improves considerably with practice. When solving an anagram it is always useful to look for common word endings such as ING, LESS, ABLE, ED, ER, LE, and common letter combinations such as SS, EN, IS or ARR.

Many solvers find it very useful to arrange the letters in a circle so that it is easier to identify possible word patterns. Others prefer to arrange the consonants in a row followed by the vowels as this enables them to spot a possible consonant sequence in which the vowels can be slotted in.

Another useful method of practice is by the use of tiles to familiarise yourself with the various pattern-detection processes. Either use Scrabble tiles for this process, alternatively make your own out of cardboard squares. Then try spelling out words with the tiles, then jumble them up and look for new words or phrases. After a relatively short period you may be surprised at how proficient you are becoming, not only at solving anagrams but inventing them yourself.

Now try the following puzzles, all thirty of which are all on an anagram based theme.

1. Anagram Theme

Pair a word from **List A** with a word from **List B** until you have three pairs, each of which is an anagram of something on the same theme. For example, if the word *shut* was in List A and the word *yard* was in List B, they could be paired together to form an anagram of *Thursday* (shut yard), and the theme could be days of the week.

List A	List B
robot	croon
ant	men
acid	relic

Clue: hit the right note

2. Managra

The shortest word in the English language from which the words *mar*, *am* and *far* can be separately produced is *farm*.

What is the shortest word in the English language from which all the following words can be separately produced?

article, castle, charity

Clue: the word you are looking for does not repeat a letter

3. Enigmagram

The four eight- letter sea-going vessels have been jumbled. Solve the four anagrams and enter the correct words in the space below, starting at the end indicated ✳ . Then transfer the nine arrowed letters to the key anagram to find a fifth sea-going vessel (9 - letters)

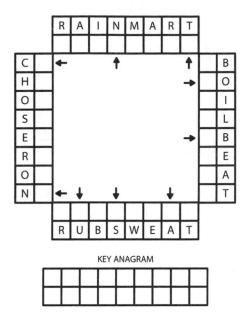

KEY ANAGRAM

4. Vegetables

Which of the following is not an anagram of a type of vegetable?

cash pin

take choir

spin rap

drain man

cult tee

war secrets

5. Find The Word

Only one of the groups of six letters below can be arranged into a 6 - letter word in the English language. Find the word.

MUTEBO

LORCIN

TABONE

HENILT

LORMTA

OFNIWE

RILBAC

6. Anagrams

Each number represents the same letter in each set. Find the six words that are all anagrams of each other.

1234

3421

3124

4213

1243

2143

7. Ouch!

Only ten letters of the alphabet do not appear in the array below.
What 10 - letter phrase (3, 2, 5) can they be arranged to spell out?

U	Z	C	W
H	K	Q	J
P	X	T	V
Y	M	G	R

Clue: Does the fakir derive any comfort from this?

8. Anagrammed Synonyms

In each of the following groups of three words your task is to find two of the three that can be paired to form an anagram of one word, which is a synonym of the word remaining. For example, LEG - MEEK - NET. The words LEG and NET are an anagram of GENTLE, which is a synonym of the remaining word - MEEK.

sorry - net - inept   sail - alike - rim

hasten - fan - suit   edit - exact - lead

able - finite - crop   lithe - sew - late

9. Liberate Tennis

Solve the anagrams in brackets (all one word) to complete the quotations by Albert Einstein.

i. (aiming at ion) is more important than knowledge.

ii. The eternal mystery of the world is its (embryonic Philistine)

iii. (tango trivia) can not be held responsible for people falling in love.

iv) Reality is merely an illusion, albeit a very (prettiness) one.

v) The most beautiful thing we can experience is the (yum stories).

10. Phrases

Solve the anagrams of familiar phrases, for example, atom slut (3, 5) clue: aggregate; answer: sum total.

i) damn genial (7, 3)   clue: top billing

ii) the piglets (5, 5)   clue: sweet dreams

iii) to undo ode (3, 3, 3)   clue: unconventional

iv) open oath (3, 1, 4)   clue: woebegone

11. Cryptagrams

The answer to each clue is an anagram to be solved within the clue, for example, device destroys the cart (7) ; answer: ratchet (anagram of *the cart*; anagram indicator; destroys)

i) Charming transformation for turbulent Gulf race (8)

ii) Literary classifier rewrites glib hair probe mystery (13)

iii) Resting houses reconstructed with high morality (13)

iv) Spin trash crazily from one vessel to another (9)

12. Antonyms

Each square contains the jumbled letters of a 9 - letter word. Find the words. The two words have opposite meanings.

13. Synonyms

Each square contains the jumbled letters of a 9 - letter word. Find the words. The two words have similar meanings.

14. Same Sound

Solve each anagram to find two phrases that are spelled differently but sound alike, as, for example, in the two phrases *a name, an aim.*

i. grape tea   **Egypt era**

ii. woken canon   **not onion**

15. Satin Stain

Insert two words that are anagrams of each other to complete the sentence, as in the example: She removed the *stain* from her new *satin* blouse.

After a fiercely competitive bout the fencing master sent his **** for ******.**

16. Palindromic Anagrams

Solve the anagrams below to, in each case, produce a short palindromic sentence, for example, opponents set = step on no pets.

sense lifeline (6, 7)

mean neon moan (4, 2, 3, 3)

overdone Denver (5, 3, 2, 4)

17. Tiny Crossword Anagram

Complete the grid so that four 4 - letter words read across and four different 4 - letter words read down by using every letter of the phrase : **raise separate arm**, once each only.

18. BRRRRRRRR

Create two related 5 - letter words using each of the ten letters of the phrase **PORN HARLOT** once each only.

19. Longest Word

What is the longest English word that can be produced from the following ten letters?

MURDOPLENH

20. When You Wish

Insert each of the letters of the phrase:

OH ! SIGNORAS

into the grid to find two connected words.

Clue: make a wish

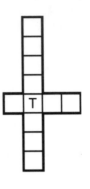

21. Numbers

Each of the following is an anagram of a number. The numbers increase in value.

For example: evens = seven

fin feet (7)

the vitrify (6, 4)

set envy (7)

to hygiene (6, 3)

yet inherent (6, 5)

herded hunter (5, 7)

shouting death (5, 8)

fill tiny room (5, 7)

22. Book Titles

Each book title is the clue to a word and the name of the book's author is an anagram of that word, for example, The Writer by A. Routh - answer: author

Confined to Bed by Sid P. Edison

My Daily Bread by Sean N. Scute

Turncoat by Pat Oates

Discriminating Palate by Meg Rout

Pigeonhole by Rosette Pye

Counter Intelligence by Angie Pose

Verbose by Ursula Gor

23. Three Of A Kind

Use each letter of the newspaper headline once each only to spell out in each case three of a kind.

Three gemstones:

Lazy Mob Departure

Three fruit:

Paper Pager Plea

Three animals:

No Lithosphere Lane

24. Countries

Which of the following is not an anagram of a country?

and ionise

lizard newts

big Laura

saw nothing

regain tan

25. Animals

Solve the anagram in brackets, each is a one-word answer, to complete the name of the breed of animal, for example, (need bare) Angus = Aberdeen Angus

(main Santa) possum

(cat brain) camel

(sheer Soho) bat

(lame ashy) terrier

(pure aeon) bison

(preen any) mountain dog

(panto again) cavy

(shirt scam) beetle

26. Footprint

Solve the four anagrams, all are one-word answers, and then say what the four words have in common.

if yard   an slid   risk elk   or moan

27. Complete The Grid

Solve the eight anagrams below (all one word answers) and then fit the words into the grid with the aid of the letters already inserted:

meet Len   a Gemini   turn car   chain me

caviare   damn tea   rare ant   tear net

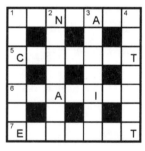

28. Famous Name Anagrams

For example: 19th-century Austrian composer (6,7) RASH SON JAUNTS

Answer: Johann Strauss

a. American singer born 1942 in Brooklyn, New York (6,9)

DARN RABBI STARES

b. Portuguese navigator and explorer (9,8)

DAMN FINE LARGE LAND

c. American tennis player born 1970 and winner of several major championships (5,6)

DRAIN SEA GAS

d. Legendary female aviator born in Achison, Kansas in 1898 (6,7)

MAIL EARTH AREA

e. 20th-century German politician, known as der alte or the old man (6,8)

ROUND NAKED AREA

f. Operatic tenor who was given the nickname the man with the orchid-lined voice   (6,6)

RANCOROUS ICE

g. American Civil War general and indian fighter (6,9,6)

CURSE STRONGER MORTGAGE

h. Italian-English author of novels such as The Sea Hawk (1915) and Captain Blood (1936) (6,8)

A FATAL SIBERIAN

i. 18th-century American statesman, scientist, inventor and writer (8,8)

BLANK INNER FIN JAM

j. Wayward woman who is the central character of Somerset Maugham's novel Rain (5,8)

THESPIANS DOOM

29. Anagram Crossword

Complete the crossword with seven-letter words. Each clue is an anagram of the word to be inserted.

Across:

1. thrones   3. sane Jim   5. be march   6. he Clive   7. see clip

10. a ale keg   13. neat boy   15. idle mop   19. harm Sal   20. needs CD

21. conical   22. new hero   23. air fern   24. duly ran

Down:

1. cosy tie   2. runs rye   3. live Jan   4. meet Len   8. the earl

9. bush lip   11. casters   12. rare nag   14. germ lab   16. in place

17. iron lad   18. dye gift

30. The Good, The Bad And The Ugly

The three clues refer to a synonym, an antonym and an anagram (*in no particular order*). Figure out the answer word in each case.

For example: halt, post, start

Answer word : stop: post(anagram), halt (synonym), start (antonym)

resumed, unnoticed, ended

fade, shimmer, singlet

thoughtful, desecration, negligent

singer, quit, enlist

base, drain, top

restful, placate, agitate

learning, illiteracy, cautioned

mental, rejoice, bewail

abundance, thread, insufficiency

III - Crosswords

Introduction:

All I did was to take an idea as old as language and modernise it by the introduction of black squares. No one is more surprised at its amazing popularity.
Arthur Wynne

Although some claim its origins date back to China 8000 years ago, it is accepted that the modern crossword puzzle was the invention of Arthur Wynne.

Wynne, who was born in Liverpool, England, was responsible for the fun section of the New York World and, on Sunday, 21 December 1913, he introduced his new innovation, a diamond-shaped word-cross puzzle.

Wynne's idea caught on immediately and the passion for crosswords quickly spread throughout America. Crosswords were seen as a perfect escape and as an intellectual stimulant. They began to appear more and more in newspapers and magazines, and the Baltimore and Ohio railroads began supplying all their main-line trains with dictionaries for its addicts.

In 1924 the idea eventually came to Britain when the first British crossword, compiled by C.W.Shepard, appeared in the *Sunday Express*, and the crossword was said to have finally *arrived* when *The Times* began its own version in 1930.

There are two basic crossword puzzle types, one having straightforward synonym type clues and one having cryptic clues. A synonym type clue is a straightforward description of the answer, for example, resting place for a bird (5); answer: perch. The cryptic clue is a puzzle in its own right and can come in many forms, and we will deal with this type of clue later in this chapter.

In all types of crossword the number in parenthesis indicates the number of letters in the answer. If you see two or more numbers then the answer is more than one word, for example, Hyde Park Corner would appear as (4, 4, 6) and down-at-heel would appear as (4-2-4).

The first seven crosswords in this chapter have all straightforward clues and the last four are cryptic type crosswords.

1. Word-Cross Puzzle

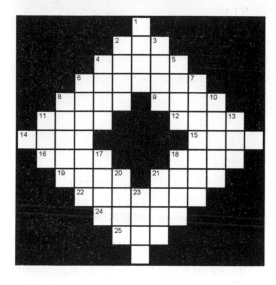

The grid shown is the exact design of that used by Arthur Wynne in his original
puzzle from December 1913, but the clues and answers are entirely different
as they have been newly compiled for this book.

Across:

2. large body of salt water (3)
4. hidden accumulation (5)
6. one thousand thousand (7)
8. step through water (4)
9. cry of suffering or distress (4)
11. enclosure with bars (4)
12. moderately fast gait of a horse (4)
14. wise man (4)
15. damage beyond repair (4)
16. incline (4)
18. crown of the head (4)
19. remain (4)
21. profane utterance (4)
22. adapt for voices or instruments (7)
24. piece of furniture (5)
25. purchase (3)

Down:

1. large sea mammal (4)
2. flatfish caught for food (4)
3. opera solo (4)
4. conceal (4)
5. simpleton (4)
6. deep purplish red (7)
7. relate a story (7)
8. emolument (5)
10. direction to the right of sunrise (5)
11. feline (3)
13. make fast and secure (3)
17. small pointed missile (4)
18. single leaf of a book (4)
20. take by a sudden grasp (4)
21. adjective meaning alone in its class (4)
23. touch along a border (4)

Across:

1. tower attached to a mosque (7)
7. depart (2)
8. have an obligation to pay (3)
10. acquiesce (6)
13. preposition used to indicate a point in time or space (2)
14. large formal dance (4)
15. long, narrow flat-bottomed boat (4)
17. protection or sponsorship (5)
18. cuts off tops of trees (4)
20. repeated word in the French phrase meaning a private conversation (4)
22. to or towards the inside (2)
24. frightened (6)
25. terribly English beverage (3)
27. in a high position (2)
28. colourless, odourless flammable gas (7)

Down:

2. former South American empire (4)
3. eternal (7)
4. straight slender stick (3)
5. in the direction of (2)
6. came to rest (7)
9. sickly or pale (3)
10. competence (7)
11. applaud (4)
12. inscription in memory of a dead person (7)
16. operator (4)
19. a single thing (3)
21. small sea gull (4)
24. sever (3)
26. first person singular of be (2)

Across:

2. reeled from side to side (9)
7. roster (4)
8. paved area (5)
9. cook with fat or oil (3)
10. low in tone (4)
11. old-timer (7)
14. submissive (6)
15. order not to do something (6)
16. senior commissioned army officer (7)
19. orderly and clean (4)
20. having existed a long time (3)
21. peak (5)
22. tall bulbous flowering plant (4)
23. with highly refined grace (9)

Down:

1. exhibiting sorrow or misery (9)
2. hard transparent blue precious stone (7)
3. now in operation (6)
4. phantasm (5)
5. direct or send to another person (5)
6. senior member of a body or profession (5)
12. erratically (8)
13. friendly (8)
15. display ostentatiously (6)
16. dwarf of folklore (5)
17. push gently (5)
18. ballroom dance of Cuban origin (5)

Across:

3. walk conceitedly (7)
7. cause to break up (6)
8. consume food (3)
9. total up (3)
10. reverent regard (6)
11. horseman in a bullfight (7)
13. probable (6)
14. 51st state of the US (6)
15. cattle thief (7)
18. small compartment for household utensils (6)
20. implement used to propel a boat (3)
21. leguminous vegetable (3)
22. derive a solution by reasoning (6)
23. highest in rank (7)

Down:

1. building for storage of animal food (4)
2. obvious (8)
3. drowsy (6)
4. the room at the top (5)
5. fine and imposing (5)
6. distinctive feature of a robin (9)
10. side-splittingly funny (9)
12. large South American snake (8)
14. arched passageway between shops (6)
16. discarded material (5)
17. fall in standard (5)
19. every individual one (4)

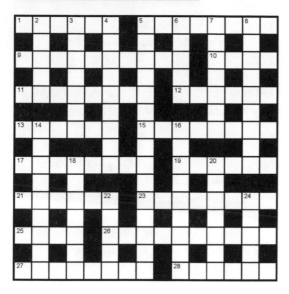

Across:

1. climbing device (6)
5. disaster (8)
9. doubting the validity of something or someone (10)
10. eat dinner (4)
11. exercises designed to increase cardiovascular fitness (8)
12. bat used in tennis (6)
13. hunting expedition in Africa (6)
15. someone who tends to hope for the best (8)
17. impressive (8)
19. flower organ that produces pollen (6)
21. empower (6)
23. readily perceived (8)
25. Icelandic story of heroic deeds (4)
26. overpoweringly light (10)
27. practise (8)
28. soft fruit used in salads (6)

Down:

2. bright, clear blue (5)
3. record of graduation or examination success (7)
4. made right (9)
5. it is staring you right in the face! (9,6)
6. someone who is defeated (5)
7. small amount (7)
8. state of the US (9)
14. something attached (9)
16. someone who tries out an aircraft in flight (4, 5)
18. hug affectionately (7)
20. a word made up of the initial letters of other words (7)
22. sea-duck with soft down (5)
24. without lighting (5)

6. The MI5 And Mr Dawe

In 1944 Europe had been at war for five long years. For some of those dark days one of the authors of this book had been a pupil at the Strand Grammar School in Tulse Hill, South London where the headmaster was a Mr L.S.Dawe.

Apart from running the school in those difficult times, Mr Dawe had time for his hobby, that of a cruciverbalist, or crossword compiler. In fact, so proficient was Mr Dawe at this hobby he became one of the regular compilers of the Daily Telegraph crossword.

Mr Dawe was also a very enterprising individual and when sentencing boys to detention, did not waste time in giving them lines to write out, but instead provided them with blank crossword grids which he asked them to fill out with words, so that later he could just add the clues and submit them to the Daily Telegraph.

It must have been a great shock to Mr Dawe, when in 1944, shortly before the invasion of France by the Allies, the school was suddenly descended upon by members of MI5 who hauled away Mr Dawe for questioning. It transpired the solution to Mr Dawe's previous days crossword in the Telegraph inexplicably contained nine words that were, in fact, key code names used in the forthcoming invasion plans.

Somehow, and just how he did it remains a mystery to this day, Mr Dawe convinced MI5 that he was not a spy and that the inclusion of the words was but a mere coincidence. After extensive questioning he was eventually released from custody.

However, it was not until 1980 that the mystery was finally unravelled when a letter appeared in the *Sunday Times* from an old boy of the school who had been a member of the crossword team. Having eventually decided that confession was good for the soul he owned up to being the culprit. It appeared that during the war his mother had been evacuated to Lincolnshire and found work in an American Air Force base. He regularly visited her at weekends and moved freely about the camp where the secret code names were often bandied about. The names had stuck with him and he had, as a result, fed them into the crossword grid.

The grid below is the actual solution that landed Mr Dawe in such deep water. The only exception is that the nine words that caused the furore have been omitted, for you to replace..

Clues to the nine solution are given below, but in no particular order. Can you complete the notorious grid?

one who is supreme above others

common name for plant of the family moraceae

city in eastern Nebraska

sharp cutting weapon with long blade

malleable yellow metallic chemical element

Roman god of the sea

Queen of the gods in Roman mythology

one of the mountain states of the US

6th June, 1944

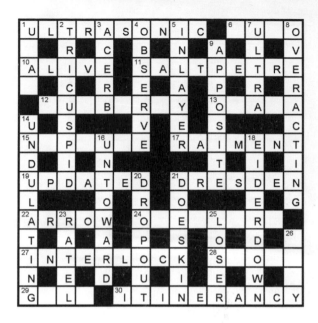

7. 12 x 12 Barred

This type of crossword is popular in many newspapers and magazines. In it there are no black squares. Instead all squares are filled with letters, and word endings/beginnings are indicated by thick black lines.

Across:

1. indigenous native (10)
11. turn from sin (6)
12. speak in an impassioned manner (5)
14. relating to the eye (7)
15. poem of fourteen lines (6)
16. waves that break onto the shore (4)
17. propel oneself in water (4)
19. simmered (6)
20. German-born American physicist (8)
24. one who doubts the existence of God (8)
26. range of mountains with rugged peaks (6)
27. jest (4)
29. compel (4)
31. city and seaport of central Italy (6)
33. British sculptor of Russian-Polish descent (7)
34. monarchy of southern Asia (5)
35. capital of Rwanda (6)
36. outwardly (10)

Down:

2. beneath (5)
3. orifice (7)
4. bridle for controlling an animal (4)
5. put in (6)
6. impressive (8)
7. musical tone (4)
8. ascended (6)
9. ogler (6)
10. not being honest with yourself (4-6)
13. evaluation (10)
18. less than zero (8)
21. showing indifference to pain (7)
22. folded material used when dressing a baby (6)
23. the amount prior to revenue deductions (6)
25. fountainhead (6)
28. the toll of a bell (5)
30. cloth made of pressed wool and fur (4)
32. prefix meaning one million (4)

I may not mean what I say, but I must say what I mean

D.S. McNutt (1902-71) - Ximenes of the Observer

For many people, the more difficult type of crossword makes use of cryptic clues. These require the solver to understand the different forms in which these clues can be presented, for example, as a play on words, an anagram, an abbreviation or a key word.

Several books have attempted to explain the use of such clues and these can, initially, be very useful. But the real learning is *hands on* experience. The more you practise on this type of crossword, the more proficient you become and eventually you will feel sufficiently confident to progress to the more difficult cryptic crosswords in newspapers such as the Daily Telegraph and The Times.

As you practise you will learn to recognise the various styles and tricks of the different compilers. Indeed where some newspapers have several different compilers, regular solvers are able to recognise which compiler has set the clues for the crossword they are attempting, just by the style of clues. They are able to get onto the same wavelength and, to a great extent, into the mind of that compiler. Such aficionados will complete the most difficult of crosswords within several minutes, while the rest of us are still scratching our heads over the first clue.

In general every cryptic clue will contain somewhere in it a definition of the answer you are seeking, or, in fact, the whole clue may sometimes be the definition. Apart from this many such clues include tricks in an attempt to lead the solver off on the wrong direction. What the solver needs to concentrate on is deconstructing the clue and analysing the separate parts within it.

In order to familiarise readers, who are not already familiar with cryptic crosswords, with the more common forms of wordplay used, several examples are listed below.

Double Meanings or Double Definition:

The clue is usually split into two parts, with each part leading to the same answer.

Example 1:

a large glass for the acrobat (7)

answer: tumbler; a tumbler is a large glass, and a tumbler is an acrobat

Example 2:

the correct direction (5)

answer: right; correct = right, direction = right

Example 3:

monument for the most sombre person (10)

answer: gravestone; gravest one = most sombre person, gravestone = monument

Anagrams:

The clue will still contain a definition, however, within the clue is an anagram of the solution and a disguised anagram indicator which will tell you which words need rearranging to obtain the answer.

There are many words that are used as anagram indicators, in fact far too many to list, however, a few such words are:

adapt	muddled	unusual	juggle
peculiar	terrible	manoeuvre	design
engineer	different	convert	awful
change	amend	mad	mysterious
mince	incorrect	dubious	repair

Example1:

ape's raid spoiled divine abode (8)

answer: paradise; ape's raid = anagram of paradise, spoiled = anagram indicator, divine abode = definition.

Example 2:

hoodlum repairs speed road (9)

answer: desperado; speed road = anagram of desperado, repairs = anagram indicator, hoodlum = definition

---

Example 3:

Tom's train seat rearranged for the man in charge (13)

answer: stationmaster; Tom's train seat = anagram of stationmaster, rearranged = anagram indicator, man in charge = definition

Example 4:

killers rent Rome taxis in confusion (13)

answer: exterminators; rent Rome taxis = anagram of exterminators, in confusion = anagram indicator, killers = definition

Hidden Answers:

The clue always contains a definition, but also an indicator that the answer is hidden within the other part of the clue, either backwards or forwards.

Example 1:

a bad dose may be found to come in a hot flush (3)

answer: flu; hidden answer = a hot (**flu**)sh, a bad dose = definition, found to come in = indicator.

Example 2:

some beastly direction (4)

answer: east, hidden answer = b**east**ly, direction = definition, some = indicator

Example 3:

sociobiologist returned African language (3)

answer: ibo, hidden answer = sociob**iolo**gist (ibo in reverse), African language = definition, returned = indicator

Split Words:

The answer is defined and one part of the answer goes inside or outside the other. An indicator is also provided.

Example 1:

Fifty-one in a party of soldiers, very sordid! (7)

answer: squalid; definition, very sordid = squalid, in = indicator, hidden answer = squa(li)d, fifty-one = LI in Roman numerals, inside squad, a party of soldiers.

Example 2:
offering a present of French wine in carriage (6)
Answer: giving; definition = offering a present, indicator = in, hidden answer = giving, vin = French wine, inside gig, a carriage.

Homophones:

Homophones are words, or even phrases, that sound like each other, but are spelled differently. Examples are son/sun, loot/lute, grey tape/great ape.

Clues which use homophones have a definition, an indicator, for example, *sounds like*, *we hear*, and a description of the homophone itself.

Example 1
Sounds as though it's a ring for the young swan (6)
Answer: cygnet; definition = young swan, indicator = sounds as though, homophone, signet = type of ring

Example 2 (this one is especially cryptic)
sounds like quite a task for this mammal with the right accent (8)
answer: aardvark; definition = mammal, indicator = sounds like (with right accent), homophone = hard work (quite a task)

Pure Cryptics:

Some such clues are designed to amuse the solver as in the famous examples:

hijklmno (answer: water - h to o - h_2o),
gsge (scrambled eggs),
bar of soap (Rovers Return - the public house or bar in the soap Coronation Street).

Other examples of pure cryptic are:

urban quarter, the home of cups and saucers = Chinatown
study computer data in the garden = read out
ancient clock may have seen it all before = old timer
might it bounce in the post office? = rubber stamp
does this American songbird like a frolic in the field? = meadowlark
enduring, like waiting for a bus that never comes = long-standing
does this marauder of the deep like lazing in the sun? = basking shark
charge for some cutlery and get the bird = spoonbill
how you were caught with your paw in the paint pot = red handed

The above is by no means the complete list of all the types of clues used by compilers of cryptic crosswords, nevertheless, it should give you some idea of the main types of clues you are likely to encounter, and some indication of the type of thought processes and often lateral thinking that needs to be employed in order to find the correct solution.

The final four crosswords in this section are all cryptic type crosswords which use many of the devices described above.

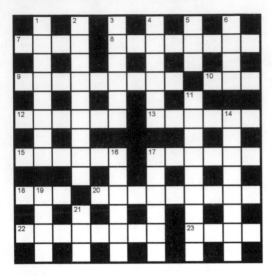

Across:

7. burden placed on us together (4)
8. reason badly before taking some tea, then reverberate (8)
9. strange period hat for a love-goddess (9)
10. bird to cut the mustard down under (3)
12. pivot after sunset and cry fretfully (6)
13. toss rice to stimulate 9 across (6)
15. brook for master to splash around in (6)
17. spinster becomes lackadaisical when bringing up the rear (6)
18. insect confused, as always, in gooseberry bush (3)
20. provide amusement or show hospitality (9)
22. chop mince, how? Chinese style (4,4)
23. garden may have delighted former Prime minister (4)

Down:

1. host's nap spoiled holiday memory (8)
2. alienated red agents (9)
3. bassinet to rock baby (6)
4. repeat poor assortment to transmit sleeping sickness (6)
5. tipsy girl found in Crown and Anchor (3)
6. feature in arithmetic reversal (4)
11. elected group put in custody with short snigger (9)
14. intuitive guess may be quite impressive (8)
16. a gentleman is around the Princess Royal with a certain style (6)
17. feeling sorrow in urge, unusually (6)
19. reverberation for a Greek nymph (4)
21. overwhelming wonder returned by Stonewall (3)

9. Cryptic Crossword !I

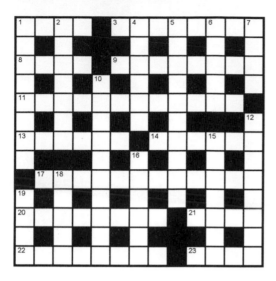

Across:

1. zero return signals end for Simenon (4)
3. largely lugubrious hat (8)
8. domesticated or uninspiring (4)
9. lilac bib marred sacred writings (8)
11. decoratively in normally neat fashion (12)
13. buoyant launch of commercial enterprise (6)
14. repress emotions when container is up (6)
17. run base alone, it becomes all so preposterous (12)
20. Roman tax collector now pulls the pints (8)
21. calumniate with indistinct articulation (4)
22. jazz on a Monday morning (3, 5)
23. devoted with love (4)

Down:

1. chase to unseat Ian Talon (8)
2. a token in name only (7)
4. Far Eastern soccer team? (6)
5. deadly nightshade destroyed Lebanon lad (10)
6. go beyond forty, I hear (5)
7. unique and, in part, fondly (4)
10. poor Miriam comes with the wrong tale, but it's all quite inconsequential (10)
12. run through with funeral vehicle bringing up the rear (8)
15. orchestral bells (7)
16. tea set neatly arranged in manor (6)
18. occupant for 16 down (5)
19. place for fussy pots (4)

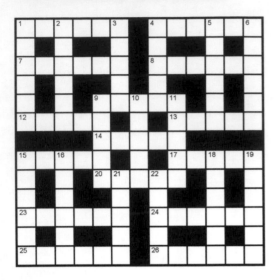

Across:

1. rainbow goddess ends predicament (6)
4. execute a prison sentence, for example (6)
7. chicory a strange requirement around four (6)
8. he sounds reveille to confuse action of house thief (6)
9. plane makes crash landing in Himalayan region (5)
12. bad accent around polar region for
quick splash round (5)
13. duck down (5)
14. spacious residence with soccer team (5)
15. pleasurable lip movement (5)
17. South African boy eats his greens (5)
20. respond regarding performance (5)
23. swig, or absorb and confuse computer giant at first (6)
24. haul popular U.K. drink over the coals (6)
25. ancient Persian king splits twenty (6)
26. dormant talent (6)

Down:

1. Gaius Julius or Sid (6)
2. club for a gymnast (6)
3. display of emotion in field of interest (5)
4. viperine snake (5)
5. pondered over warmed spirit (6)
6. paralysed with fear when struck (6)
9. repeated refusal in imaginary land (5)
10. tight-fitting jacket in double-time (5)
11. strange tales in the slightest degree (5)
15. strange Egyptian riddle (6)
16. display unnatural bias or express pressure (6)
18. vegetable out on a limb for starters (6)
19. side-track some undertakers around four (6)
21. short odds (5)
22. calcereous polypary (5)

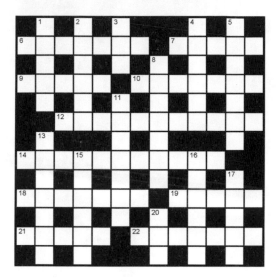

Across:

6. accept delivery, perhaps illegally (7)
7. coy identification for little Timothy (5)
9. poem written between thousands achieves the right connection into cyberspace (5)
10. sharing around to embellish (7)
12. the Ratty Quails have just what it takes with new line-up (4, 7)
14. Biblical duo disorientated normally balanced Ian (4, 3, 4)
18. I rob duo, then inexplicably visit the ladies chamber (7)
19. spruce up the husband-to-be (5)
21. principle doctrine, either way you look at it (5)
22. plates of meat and mince pies (7)

Down:

1. courageous man taken to polar region to view wading bird (5)
2. acquiesce regarding period of fasting (6)
3. clinging lady spotted fleetingly in ivory tower (3)
4. skirt for alpine peasant woman (6)
5. arrange her suit, it's rough and hairy, I hear (7)
8. pure native (7)
11. at one's wit's end, it's with all the worry (7)
13. hereditary title spoiled one brat (7)
15. bowed head in assent and grabbed forty winks (6)
16. exclamation curtailed a bath (6)
17. bread or moolah, colloquially (5)
20. confused enemy in three-four time (3)

IV – Crossword Variations

Introduction:

There are many puzzles which are variations, or spin-offs, on the traditional crossword puzzle. Several such examples are included in this chapter.

1. X-Word Search

This puzzle consists of a traditional crossword puzzle combined with a word search puzzle.

All the answers to the crossword clues can also be found in the word-search grid, reading horizontally, vertically, diagonally, backwards, forwards, up or down, but always in a straight line.

It is your choice whether you treat the crossword and word-search as two separate puzzles, or use the word-search in order to assist you in completing the crossword.

T	N	A	L	I	A	S	S	A	N
F	S	Q	S	B	K	S	O	L	D
L	E	E	W	A	Y	O	S	X	I
I	R	E	D	D	U	Z	A	E	S
G	D	R	N	O	F	C	E	L	T
H	W	G	E	S	M	S	E	P	A
T	U	A	T	L	S	K	A	I	Y
M	T	U	N	B	I	D	C	L	H
M	D	S	I	I	A	M	H	F	H
Y	S	L	E	B	P	K	S	V	Z

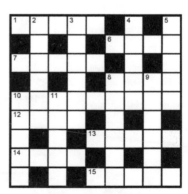

Clue numbers refer to crossword grid:

Across:

1. facial expression of pleasure
6. merchandised
7. source of milk in cattle
8. turn over quickly or many times
10. attacker
12. remain
13. be of the same opinion
14. every individual one
15. examine carefully

Down:

2. humble
3. enough space for free movement
4. furry Australian animal
5. adjust for new use
8. a series of stairs
9. propose
10. valuable possession
11. dressing for salads or meats

2. Crossjig

Piece the crossword together.

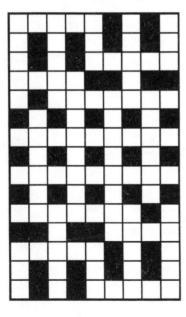

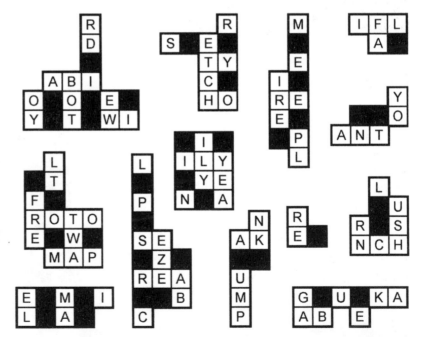

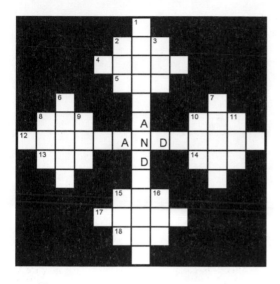

All clues are given except 1 down and 12 across. Find the answers to the missing clues by solving the other clues. You will find that the solutions both 1 down and 12 across consist of two five-letter words that form familiar phrases when connected by the word **and.**

Across:

2. unit of electrical resistance
4. loose outer garment
5. lacking moisture
8. large primate
10. implement used to propel a boat
13. encountered
14. risk money on an outcome
15. nocturnal bird of prey
17. rate of motion
18. beverage made from cured leaves

Down:

2. venerable
3. be likely to
6. watched secretly
7. area allotted to women in a Muslim household
8. upper limb
9. consume
10. sphere
11. decompose
15. choose
16. meadow

Reconstruct the crossword in the right-hand grid. In the left-hand grid all the vowels are in the correct position but all the consonants are in the wrong position. There is one capitalised name reading downwards, which is the name of a country.

 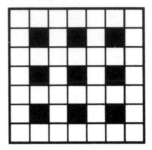

5. Words In Circulation

All answers are six-letter words and may circulate either clockwise or anti-clockwise round their respective number.

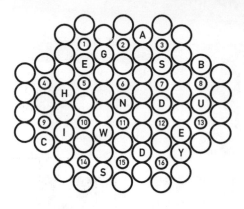

Clues:

1. rush forward in an assault
3. attack violently
5. to keep safe from danger or attack
7. carriage for sliding on snow
9. disastrous or appalling
11. move about aimlessly
13. evaded
15. harebrained

2. thick oily material or fat
4. the 50th state of the US
6. folklore
8. lacking capability
10. cutting tool or type of puzzle
12. interfere
14. regulate or alter
16. indefinitely large number

6. Alphabet Crossword

Insert the 26 letters of the alphabet once each only in order to complete the crossword.

**A B C D E F G H I J K L M
N O P Q R S T U V W X Y Z**

A daffynition is an alternative punning dictionary, for example:
kindred = a fear of relatives,
minimum = a short parent,
illegal = a big sick bird.

Try to work out the words from the daffynitions given, alternate letters of the answer are given, and then insert the answers into the correct position in the grid with the help of the initial letters already entered.

Clues:

a guard singing Bach	* E * T * I * U * A *
a bomb in a parrot	* O * I * I * S
Asian jewellery	* R * E * T * E * I * G
hooker's fee	* A * T * A * E
how the cannibal felt about his mother-in-law	* L * D * A * O *
an advocate of SI units	* R * G * A * M *
what one should be in genteel company	* X * R * P * L * T *
a devilish stretch of water	* E * O * S * R * T *
a USA campaign slogan in the 1980s	* L * C * R * N
keep the door ajar	* R * P * G * T *

8. Missing Consonants

Insert the consonants provided in order to complete the crossword.

T M T T Z X M R R R R C N N G

9. Fivers

Insert all the 5-letter words into the grid to complete the crossword.

psalm	total	sheep
amend	elvan	cheer
other	inane	pagan
nexus	adapt	usher
muted	tidal	exist
enrol	otter	adult
noted	tacit	eaten
trade	count	alarm
ousel	apron	urban
above	equip	close
giant	expel	terse
inept	igloo	eerie

Insert the 26-letters of the alphabet into the grid once each only in order to complete the crossword.

**A B C D E F G H I J K L M
N O P Q R S T U V W X Y Z**

Clues are given to the eight words to be inserted, but in no particular order.

Clues:

lively dance
drowsy or stupid
muddy and sticky
mammal, or clever person
large barrel-shaped container
cause to become crinkled
pronoun used as a group that includes the speaker
money institutions

V – Acrostics

Introduction:

The traditional acrostic is a composition, usually in the form of a poem, in which the initial letters of the lines taken in order spell out a word or short sentence.

The word *acrostic* is derived from the Latin word *acrostichis* which is a composite of two Greek words *akron* (end) and *stiikhos* (line of verse). Acrostics are of ancient origin and examples appear throughout history.

In modern times, acrostics have been presented in books and magazines as puzzles with crossword type clues, and it is this type of puzzle on which we will concentrate in this section.

As in the example below, a number of clues are given below the main grid. The answers are then entered in the box opposite each clue and then transferred to the main grid according to the code above each letter. When all the clues have been solved and all the letters transferred to the main grid the answer, usually a quotation, will appear.

	a	b	c	d	e	f	g	h	i
1	F	I	N	D		T	H	E	
2	Q	U	O	T	A	T	I	O	N

Clues:

i. trust, belief or religion

ii. bend the head as a sign of assent

iii. the number resulting from division

Answer Boxes:

1a	2e	2g	1f	1g
F	A	I	T	H

1c	2c	1d
N	O	D

2a	2b	2h	2d	1b	1h	2i	2f
Q	U	O	T	I	E	N	T

As can be seen, above the letter F, for example, is the code 1a, therefore, F is entered in the main grid in the column under the letter **a** and the line opposite the number **1**.

The five puzzles which follow are the same format as the above example, however, in addition the first letter of each answer will spell out the name of the author of the quotation.

	a	b	c	d	e	f	g	h	i
1									
2									
3									
4									
5									
6									
7									

Solve the clues, enter the answers in the box opposite, then transfer the letters of the answer to the main grid according to the code above it, and a quotation will be revealed. The first letter of each answer will spell out the author of the quotation.

For example 2c means that the letter is entered in the main grid in the line opposite the number 2 and in the column below the letter c.

Clues:

i. reveal or demonstrate

ii. something peculiar

iii. demanding or exacting

iv. annulled or repealed

v. having no company

vi. very small

vii. locomotive or machine

viii. a performance by just one person

Answer Boxes:

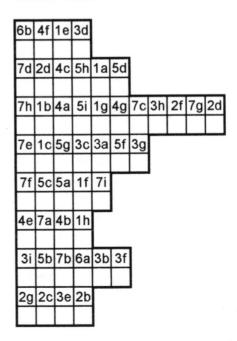

	a	b	c	d	e	f	g	h	i	j	k
1											
2											
3											
4											
5											
6											

Solve the clues, enter the answers in the box opposite, then transfer the letters of the answer to the main grid according to the code above it, and a quotation will be revealed. The first letter of each answer will spell out the author of the quotation.

For example 2c means that the letter is entered in the main grid in the line opposite the number 2 and in the column below the letter c.

Clues:

i. carrot, radish, cabbage, for example

ii. possess

iii. radiation that makes vision possible

iv. held very firmly

v. fuss

vi. Christopher *********, writer whose *I am a Camera* was adapted for the musical *Cabaret*.

vii. obtain repairs or fresh supplies

viii. trapped in a net

Answer Boxes:

5i	1i	3g	1c	3c	5h	1e	4c	4i

4g	4a	3f

4d	3e	1g	5g	1a

1k	1f	1h	3d	5d

2d	4f	2i

6f	5b	1b	2b	2j	2c	6b	5e	6a

2a	4b	2h	5a	6g

5j	4h	1j	6c	3a	2c	6d	2f

	a	b	c	d	e	f	g	h	i	j	k	l
1												
2												
3												
4												
5												
6												

Solve the clues, enter the answers in the box opposite, then transfer the letters of the answer to the main grid according to the code above it, and a quotation will be revealed. The first letter of each answer will spell out the author of the quotation.

For example 2c means that the letter is entered in the main grid in the line opposite the number 2 and in the column below the letter c.

Clues:

i. what money is when in arrears

ii. blockhead or blunder

iii. daily record of personal experiences

iv. period of time associated with something

v. regular publication reporting recent events

vi. period between dusk and dawn

vii. grown-up person

viii alone

ix lift

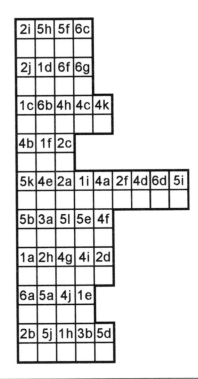

	a	b	c	d	e	f	g	h	i	j	k	l
1												
2												
3												
4												
5												
6												

Solve the clues, enter the answers in the box opposite, then transfer the letters of the answer to the main grid according to the code above it, and a quotation will be revealed. The first letter of each answer will spell out the author of the quotation.

For example 2c means that the letter is entered in the main grid in the line opposite the number 2 and in the column below the letter c.

Clues:

i. a striking or spectacular exhibition

ii. establish a strong position

iii. not in any place

iv. tuition

v. wide, full, taking in much

vi. quartz with bands of various colours

Answer Boxes:

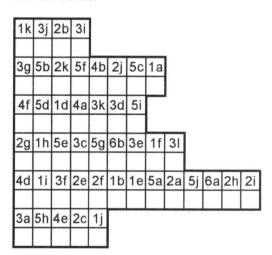

Solve the clues, enter the answers in the box opposite, then transfer the letters of the answer to the main grid according to the code above it, and a quotation will be revealed. The first letter of each answer will spell out the author of the quotation.

For example 2c means that the letter is entered in the main grid in the line opposite the number 2 and in the column below the letter c.

	a	b	c	d	e	f	g	h	i	j	k	l	m
1													
2													
3													
4													

Clues:

i. mathematical statement that two things are equal

ii. public houses

iii. adverb used to make a statement negative

iv. blemish

v. fitting close together

vi. someone with an exaggerated sense of self-importance

vii. demon, or mischievous child

viii. direction to the left of someone facing east

Answer Boxes:

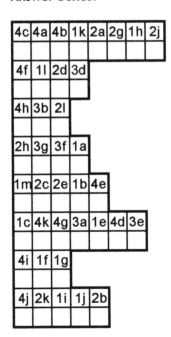

VI – Codes And Cryptograms

Introduction:

Cryptography is the alteration of the form of a message by codes and ciphers to conceal its meaning. A cryptogram is the coded message, and cryptoanalysis is the breaking of the codes or cipher without the key.

The simplest cryptograms are those in which every letter of the alphabet from A to Z (known as the plain text) is substituted for another in the coded text, for example, the letter A might be substituted by the letter Q and the letter B might be substituted by the letter K. This substitution may be random, as in the case of the puzzles which appear later in this section, or it may be to a pattern, for example where A is substituted by C, B is substituted by D and C is substituted by E. This type of substitution is known as the Caesar shift after the Roman emperor Julius Caesar who is reputed to have devised this code.

Cryptoanalysts have at their disposal a great deal of information such as letter and word frequency. The latest information on the order in which letters appear most frequently in the English language is ETAOINSHR, and the full list of the twenty-six letters of the alphabet together with their associated percentages is as follows:

a	8.2	n	6.7
b	1.5	o	7.5
c	2.8	p	1.9
d	4.3	q	0.1
e	12.7	r	6.0
f	2.2	s	6.3
g	2.0	t	9.1
h	6.1	u	2.8
i	7.0	v	1.0
j	0.2	w	2.4
k	0.8	x	0.2
l	4.0	y	2.0
m	2.4	z	0.1

The order in which letters appear most often at the beginning of a word is TAOSTWHCB and at the end ESDTNRYO.

So, armed which such a wealth of information, how does one go about decoding a simple substitution cryptogram, that is, one in which each letter of the alphabet has been substituted for another?

By far the easiest ones to deal with are those that contain a four-letter word which begins and ends with the same letter, for example JDBJ. There is an extremely good chance this is the word THAT, which should then enable you to discover the word THE, and now you are well on your way to solving the cryptogram.

If the word THAT does not appear, then try to work out what might be the letter E and pencil this in lightly under the coded text throughout the cryptogram. Then look for single letter words which will usually either be A or I, and a repeated three-letter word ending, possibly ING - the most common three-letter ending in the English language. Also look for other obvious words such as AND, and the most common two-letter word in the English language - OF. Also try to identify double letters - EE, FF, LL, OO, RR and SS are the most common, and four-letter endings such as LESS and NESS..

Now try the following which are all simple substitution cryptograms, in which each letter of the alphabet has been substituted at random for another.

* indicates a capitalised word within the coded text

Question 1

QOEQKYQHRQ   UF   D   CKQDP   DGUDHPDCQ.   PNQ

EKVJXQA   UF   PNDP   BNQH   LVI   CQPPNQ   QOEQKYQHRQ

LVI   DKQ   PVV   VXG   PV   GV   DHLPNYHC   DJVIP   YP

WYAAL   RVHHVKF

Question 2

I JIW XV I VEGGHVV XY KH CHAV ET XW

AKH JFLWXWC IWQ CHAV AF RHQ IA WXCKA,

IWQ XW RHADHHW KH QFHV DKIA KH DIWAV

AF QF

RFR QNSIW

Question 3

EMAAJGGYY - S WVMNZ MK ZYMZPY CBM

JIQJHJQNSPPO ESI QM IMGBJIW LNG SX S WVMNZ

QYEJQY GBSG IMGBJIW ESI LY QMIY

KVYQ SPPYI

Question 4

NPMO XJL MDOG DZ ZCGBY YLRDBT YX ODBW

ZXIGYNDBT YX WX ADYN YNG YDIG AG NPQG

LJZNGW YNLXJTN MDOG YLRDBT YX ZPQG

ADMM LXTGLZ

QVJ'W   EVNNS   IHVBW   WCD   EVNXQ   TVAGJM   WV

IJ   DJQ   WVQIS.   GW'O   IXNDIQS   WVAVNNVE   GJ

*IBOWNIXGI

TCINXDO   OTCBXWF

SHIBMYL   HI   BSJ   QJYIHMG   MU   OPIB   JQJGBI   BSPB

OJMOAJ   SPQJ   FJZHFJF   BM   PEYJJ   WOMG

GPOMAJMG   NMGPOPYBJ

Now to take the above one stage further, what if the sender of the message wishes to convey a further message in the same cryptogram. This is done by the addition of keywords, which may be hidden in the plain or the keyed text. The following puzzle is an illustration of this method of cryptography.

7. Cryptokey

Start by solving the cryptogram that follows, which is a straightforward code in which each letter of the alphabet has been replaced by another.

JIXRSJK   SH   LH   GLHC   LH   SX   NIIUH.   GZGFCXRSJK   XLUGH

NIJK   GF   XRLJ   CIY   GBEGPX.   SQ   LJCXRSJK   PLJ   KI   AFIJK,

SX   ASNN   MI   HI;   LJM   LNALCH   LX   XRG   AIFHX   EIHHSONG

VIVGJX.

VYFERC'H   NLA

Now try to find a keyed phrase (5 - 2 - 10) connected with the cryptogram. Against each letter of plain text below (line 1) write its encoded form (line2). Then, against each letter of code text (line 3) write its plain text form (line 4). You will find that some letters in line 4 are in alphabetical order; the letters that are not are those that make up the key phrase. They appear in their correct order, although, of course, repeated letters have been omitted and must be replaced, for example ANPLEDY would be all that would appear of 'an apple a day'.

1 ABCDEFGHIJKLMNOPQRSTUVWXYZ

2

3 ABCDEFGHIJKLMNOPQRSTUVWXYZ

4

8. Cryptophone

Decipher the codes shown below the telephone face. Each number represents one of the letters shown with it on the telephone dial. A number does not represent the same letter each time.

STU	VWX	YZ
7	8	9

JKL	MNO	PQR
4	5	6

ABC	DEF	GHI
1	2	3

For example:

C	R	Y	P	T	O	P	H	O	N	E
1	6	9	6	7	5	6	3	5	5	2

i. Somewhere in North America:

5313161   21447

ii. A phrase

2177   152   2763577

iii. A phrase

652769   35   557355

iv. 14-letter word

15566232573142

v. An animal

41733353   4114177

vi. An event in history

7615373   13834   816

vii. Type of structure

1157342826   163232

viii. A phrase

731547   256   5573353

ix. Type of food

14114   256277   317217

x. Sporting term

721353114   45514577

xi. A phrase

4215   5826   111481627

xii. A phrase

25623552   1551477355

xiii. A phrase

5512   137725   78312   739

xiv. Historical character

155532   663512   1316432

xv. A political institution

35772   52   626627257173827

9. Strange Notice

The following notice suddenly appeared in the park. What does it mean?

S S A   R G E

H T F

FO   PE

EK

10. Disney's World

Decode the following to reveal a quotation from Walt Disney.

VF   YVV   CVN   DRVVM   VT,   YVV   CVN   DV   VT.

11. The Hidden Message

Romeo sent Kate the following secret message. What does it mean?

At a loose end

Romeo

Kate

Fort Worth

goes under

12. Ale In Cans Code

The following puzzle is based on a cipher used very successfully by Abraham Lincoln during the American Civil War. The object is to read the message paying attention to the sounds of the words, rather than their spelling, in order to reveal the real meaning.

two chain G hand two him prover tod if errant thins

13. Numbergram

This is a straight substitution cryprogram in which each letter of the alphabet has been substituted by a number corresponding to its position in the alphabet - i.e. A = 1, B = 2, etc. The problem is to find not only the starting and finishing point of the letters but of the words too. For instance, SOLVE THE CRYPTOGRAM, which is represented by the numbers 19, 15, 12, 22, 5   20, 8, 5,   3, 18, 25, 16, 20, 15, 7, 18, 1, 13 would appear as : 191512225208531825162015718113.

Now try to unravel the following quotation and author:

**20182120891913151851561192018114751820811469320915 14
131181120231914**

14. The Polybius Cipher

A	B	C	D	E
F	G	H	I	J
K	L	M	N	O
P	Q	R	S	T
U	V	W	X	Y

This code was invented by a Greek writer, Polybius, in the 2nd century BC.

With the aid of the grid above, can you crack the code and decipher the quotation below?

45, 24, 33, 15, ' 44   21, 51, 34   53, 23, 15, 34   55, 35, 51, ' 43, 15

23, 11, 52, 24, 34, 22   21, 32, 24, 15, 44

31, 15, 43, 33, 24, 45   45, 23, 15   21, 43, 35, 22

In the office, the staff were given new ID numbers.

Josephene was given 101916814

Christopher was given 3818192016818

What number was given to Margaret?

VII - Word Search

Introduction:

Word Search puzzles are popular in newspapers and magazines and as promotional competitions.

In such puzzles the requirement is to find words which are hidden in a grid. The words may appear horizontally, vertically or diagonally, backwards or forwards and up or down, but always in a straight line according to the example below.

		S	D	R	A	W	K	C	A	B	
			O					Y			
F	O	R	W	A	R	D	S	L		L	V
	L		N			L		P	A	E
		A			A			U	C	R
		N		N				I	T
L	A	T	N	O	Z	I	R	O	H	T	I
		G		G				R	C
	A		K	C	A	B		E	A
	I				I		V	L
D					D		L
H	O	R	I	Z	O	N	T	A	L	L	Y

The easiest Word Searches to solve are those where the hidden words are provided and the task is to simply find the words that have been listed. The most difficult are where you are asked to find a certain number of words or names on a certain theme, however, you are not told what these words are.

In the grid, all the squares are filled with letters, however, whilst some of the letters may be used several times for different words, not all letters may necessarily be used at all. The more words that appear diagonally, the more difficult the puzzle is to solve.

The following is a selection of five word search puzzles, each on a different theme and which gradually increase in difficulty throughout.

1. What The Dickens!

Complete the titles below, each of which is a work by Charles Dickens.

------------ Rudge

A ---------------- Carol

David ----------------

------------ Drood

Hard ----------------

Martin -------------

The -------------- Papers

The Old ---------------- Shop

Our ---------------- Friend

Sketches by --------------

The -------------- of Life

--------------- House

--------------- on the Hearth

-------------- and Son

Great ----------------

Little ----------------

Master Humphrey's ----------------

----------------- Nickleby

Oliver ----------------

----------------- Papers

A Tale of Two ----------------

The -----------------

The missing words can all be found in the grid horizontally, vertically or diagonally, backwards or forwards, up or down, but always in a straight line.

M	E	A	C	H	R	I	S	T	M	A	S	E
U	L	G	O	F	D	U	M	U	G	N	E	D
T	T	W	P	Z	O	B	W	T	O	D	I	W
U	T	K	P	M	R	L	Y	I	Y	J	T	I
A	A	P	E	R	R	E	T	W	B	S	I	N
L	B	P	R	P	I	A	I	E	A	E	C	O
M	N	K	F	I	T	K	S	L	N	M	H	L
D	X	G	I	C	E	I	O	Z	R	I	I	H
O	V	H	E	K	K	H	I	Z	A	T	M	P
M	T	P	L	W	C	P	R	U	B	W	E	M
B	X	B	D	I	I	M	U	H	I	I	S	F
E	W	G	N	C	R	L	C	C	N	S	H	C
Y	F	A	R	K	C	O	L	C	S	T	X	C

R	S	Y	M	B	I	R	D	P	N
E	T	A	L	E	L	R	N	R	O
N	A	T	I	L	O	P	A	E	N
A	G	S	E	B	H	O	L	W	A
Z	E	I	G	A	E	L	E	T	G
Z	C	L	E	T	N	I	C	N	O
I	O	K	M	S	G	S	A	A	N
P	A	V	O	N	R	H	R	X	A
I	C	C	R	O	I	V	G	O	I
L	H	U	A	C	N	X	U	N	P

The answer to each of the General Knowledge trivia questions can be found in the grid. This time there are no diagonals. The answers appear either horizontally or vertically, backwards, forwards, up or down, and always in a straight line.

i. Opera written by Richard Wagner

ii. Nine-sided figure

iii. Type of horse

iv. The longest river in Scotland

v. Painter of The Hay Wain

vi. Nationality of the composer Chopin

vii. Paul Simon's 1985 Album of the Year

viii. What type of creature is a manakin?

ix. The Albert Canal runs between which two Belgium cities?

x. What type of fabric is shantung?

xi. A type of ice-cream

xii. Location of the 1960 Olympic Games

xiii. Instrument played by jazz great Earl 'Fatha' Hines

xiv. Classic movie in which John Wayne played the Ringo Kid

E	N	E	R	U	B	N	A	V	S	M	A	D	A	F
I	J	O	A	Q	B	U	O	J	A	C	K	S	O	N
S	Y	O	T	R	S	D	G	X	B	K	S	R	K	J
E	Y	E	H	N	T	N	N	Z	I	I	D	F	E	H
N	O	T	G	N	I	H	S	A	W	N	I	F	N	H
H	B	N	M	D	S	L	U	H	L	L	F	T	N	R
O	U	U	R	U	I	O	C	R	L	E	A	S	E	E
W	S	A	C	N	N	L	N	M	R	Y	V	J	D	L
E	H	M	C	H	T	R	O	S	L	U	R	E	Y	Y
R	A	O	A	A	A	R	O	O	S	E	V	E	L	T
H	L	Y	F	D	E	N	R	E	C	R	E	I	P	C
N	E	T	P	T	I	G	A	R	F	I	E	L	D	P
S	H	A	R	R	I	S	O	N	A	M	U	R	T	O
G	R	A	N	T	H	O	O	V	E	R	T	W	A	L
F	C	M	R	E	A	G	A	N	O	S	L	I	W	K

Hidden in the grid are the surnames of 37 United States presidents.
How many can you find?

The names can all be found in the grid horizontally, vertically or diagonally, backwards or forwards, up or down, but always in a straight line.

Complete the two-word phrases below.

------ replay

------ point

above ------

------ movie

stage ------

male ------

------ robbery

word ------

------ fallacy

------ land

wine ------

------ stick

concrete ------

------ pilot

------ lily

press ------

bargain ------

------ hour

------ pen

------ trove

------ night

------ tax

------ canal

------ number

------ oath

I	B	A	L	L	P	O	I	N	T	I	Q	W	V	T
N	O	I	T	A	I	C	O	S	S	A	W	P	V	H
H	I	P	P	O	C	R	A	T	I	C	A	P	O	G
E	T	A	T	E	D	Y	T	O	N	L	K	F	B	I
R	N	T	I	S	I	E	E	D	I	B	E	E	Y	L
I	E	H	T	S	R	L	L	M	V	B	L	M	K	Y
T	M	E	N	O	E	G	E	M	U	L	E	V	X	A
A	E	T	A	R	C	N	P	I	A	K	V	D	D	D
N	S	I	H	C	T	U	H	D	H	T	E	N	I	V
C	A	C	C	A	I	J	O	S	C	S	N	O	S	A
E	B	S	R	L	O	N	N	U	I	P	T	I	A	N
Z	M	Y	E	H	N	X	E	M	N	P	H	T	S	T
J	V	N	M	A	U	T	O	M	A	T	I	C	T	A
D	T	H	C	A	O	R	P	E	R	Z	N	A	E	G
O	X	W	P	U	P	V	T	R	E	A	S	U	R	E

The missing words can all be found in the grid horizontally, vertically or diagonally, backwards or forwards, up or down, but always in a straight line.

S	A	U	D	I	A	R	A	B	I	A	B	K	U	E
Z	O	C	I	X	E	M	B	D	H	L	J	G	O	T
N	L	U	J	I	X	V	T	S	A	N	A	R	P	J
P	B	B	T	N	E	D	E	W	S	N	P	E	O	J
Z	O	A	P	H	N	D	N	N	D	E	A	E	R	W
T	L	C	R	A	A	A	E	A	E	W	N	C	T	G
Y	I	R	L	L	K	F	K	N	L	Z	D	E	U	A
T	V	N	G	Y	W	I	R	N	M	E	U	M	G	A
P	I	N	D	O	N	E	S	I	A	A	C	E	A	L
F	A	I	G	T	B	A	M	T	C	L	R	I	L	M
B	Y	A	L	M	O	R	M	I	A	A	I	K	N	A
P	N	P	H	U	N	G	A	R	Y	N	I	R	G	L
Q	E	S	U	U	Q	M	O	Z	E	D	A	J	S	I
K	K	R	J	P	A	I	D	N	I	G	E	R	I	A
E	S	W	U	J	I	Y	Z	Q	U	L	Q	B	I	F

Hidden in the grid are the names of 34 countries.
How many can you find?

The names can all be found in the grid horizontally, vertically or diagonally, backwards or forwards, up or down, but always in a straight line.

VIII – Magic Word Squares

Introduction:

A magic word square is constructed using words of equal length, so that the same words can be read both horizontally and vertically, as in the examples below.

  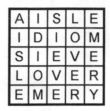

Magic word squares become progressively more difficult to compile as the number of letters in the words increases. Several 9 x 9 word squares have been constructed, however, they delve into very obscure words or proper nouns. The 10 x 10 word square has yet to be achieved, and it is unlikely that one is possible in the English language.

This section contains a number of magic word squares which are presented in a variety of ways. Included are several blended magic squares which consist of a number of separate, but interlinked squares.

The first ever blended magic squares appeared in a woman's magazine, *The People's Home Journal*, in September 1904 and a further ten examples appeared between 1904 and 1908. They consisted of five interlocked 3 x 3 magic squares, and at least eight more appeared in the companion magazine, *Good Literature*, starting in May 1905. Some puzzle experts argue that these were the world's first cross-word puzzles.

1. Blended Magic

Insert the words provided into the grid to produce four 3 x 3 magic word squares, linked with four 4 x 4 magic word squares which are in turn linked with one 5 x 5 magic word square in the centre.

3 - letter words

ego	ago
pea	err
ran	mew
eel	now
art	sea
all	won

4 - letter words

reap	palm
Abel	damp
area	saga
germ	plea
wasp	mill
aria	apex
ease	sere
army	acer

5 - letter words

radii
aided
arena
niece
edged

2. 5 x 5 Numbered

¹	²	³	⁴	⁵
⁶				
⁷				
⁸				
⁹				

Solve the clues, all the answers are five-letter words, and a magic word square will appear once the words are placed in the grid:

1 across / 1 down   tear into tiny pieces

6 across / 2 down   lift with effort

7 across / 3 down   the capital of Morocco

8 across / 4 down   manage to avoid

9 across / 5 down   discourage or prevent

3. 4 x 4 Anagram

Use all the letters of the phrase CAREFREE CAMEROON once each only to create four 4 - letter words that when placed correctly in the grid will produce a 4 x 4 magic word square in which the same four words appear both across and down

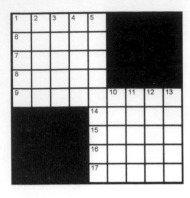

Solve the clues, all are five letter words except 9 across / 5 down, and two 5 x 5 magic word squares will appear.

1 across / 1 down	to present a role on stage
6 across / 2 down	aristocratic
7 across / 3 down	at right angles to the keel
8 across / 4 down	device for holding things together
9 across / 5 down	enticingly attractive woman (9 letters)
14 across / 10 down	establishment for raising cattle, sheep or horses
15 across / 11 down	follow as a consequence
16 across / 12 down	equipment for breathing under water
17 across / 13 down	trim wool from a sheep

5. 5 x 5 Consonants

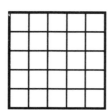

Insert the consonants provided into the grid to complete the 5 x 5 magic square in
which all five words read the same across and down.

L   P   G   G   R   R   C   L   L   C   L   T   T

6. 5 x 5 Unnumbered

The answers to the clues are all five letter words which when placed correctly in the grid will read the same across and down.

Clues (in no particular order):

persistent attack of a fortified place

excessive or abnormal enthusiasm

break into pieces

woman's part of a Mohammedan dwelling

rage

7. 5 x 5 Anagram

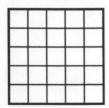

Use all the letters of the phrase ACCREDITED EASIEST DIATRIBE once each only to create five 5 - letter words that when placed correctly in the grid will produce a 5 x 5 magic word square in which the same five words appear both across and down

8. 6 x 6 Unnumbered

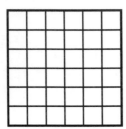

The answers to the clues are all six letter words which when placed correctly in the grid will read the same across and down.

Clues (in no particular order):

lively or energetic

referring to, especially as in a commendation

mischievous person

account book

expressed in words

take vengance for

This puzzle consists of five 4 x 4 interlocked Magic Word squares.

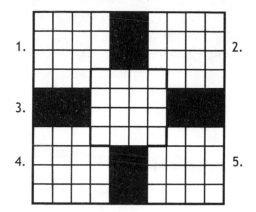

1.
2.
3.
4.
5.

Clues are given. Each set refers to a magic square as numbered, however, within each set the clues are in no particular order. Solve the clues and place the words correctly in each set to produce the five 4 x 4 magic squares.

Set 1:

repetition of sound caused by reflection of sound waves

nuisance

urban area

display

Set 2:

East Indian timber tree or its wood

otherwise

continent in the Eastern hemisphere

somewhere to sit

Set 3:

pointed device to urge on a horse

catch sight of

beginner or novice

the home of a bird

Set 4:

place where an archaelogical excavation is made

witty remark or story

a sometimes difficult expedition

native ruler in parts of Asia and Africa

Set 5:

inactive or lazy

leave out

to rain heavily

distinctive method of expression

This puzzle consists of four 4 x 4 Magic Word squares interlocked with a 6 x 6 magic word square in the middle.

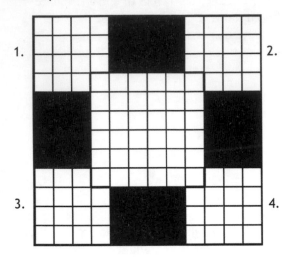

1.   2.

3.   4.

6 x 6 Magic Square

clergyman in charge of a parish
cuts into pieces
long narrow furrow in the ground
pressure or strain
complete or whole
achieved a goal in soccer

Clues are given. Each set refers to a magic square as numbered, however, within each set the clues are in no particular order. Solve the clues and place the words correctly in each set to produce the four 4 x 4 magic squares and one 6 x 6 magic square.

4 x 4 Magic Squares

Set 1

Biblical brother of Cain
list of food in a restaurant
addition sign
device for producing light

Set 2

narrow thoroughfare
afresh
fastened by stitches
cry of grief

Set 3

not changing
a sound of derision
main upright part of a plant
very small quantity

Set 4

clean or dry by rubbing
long-necked water loving bird
highest point
immediately following

IX - Lateral Thinking

Introduction:

The word *lateral* means of or relating to the side away from the median axis.

Lateral thinking is a method of solving a problem by attempting to look at that problem from many angles rather than search for a direct head-on solution. It involves, therefore, the need to think outside the box and develop a degree of creative, innovative thinking, which seeks to change our natural and traditional perceptions, concepts and ideas. By developing this type of thinking we greatly increase our ability to solve problems that face us, that we could not otherwise solve.

To solve the puzzles in this section it is necessary to think laterally and creatively and look for solutions that may not seem apparent on first inspection. These puzzles do not involve knowledge of word meanings. Instead you are looking for patterns and common traits. If you cannot solve any of these puzzles at first glance, do not rush to look up the answer, but instead return to the puzzle later to have a fresh look. Sometimes a puzzle which baffles you originally may suddenly appear soluble some hours or even days later.

1. Addition

If:

denote + existence + blowtorch = awakening

and:

solenoid + indigenous = kowtow

then does:

undergrowth + regrowth + Marxists = ?

thirty, forty, seventy or ninety ?

2. Find The Sequence

whale, kingdom, lunar, reign

which word below continues the above sequence?

rain, cloud, shower, thunder, wind

3. Find The Lady

Danube, scolds, verify

Who comes next?

Evelyn, Pamela, Agatha, Sheila, Yvonne

4. Something In Common

What do these pairs of words have in common?

lemur	alcove
scalp	snake
crock	yield
stand	espy

5. Pairs

Find a reason for pairing a word from List A with a word in List B until you have seven pairs of words all sharing the same feature.

List A	List B
Belgrade	loan
Labrador	neat
Barbados	road
Canberra	gone
Alicante	soda
Pamplona	dear
Dordogne	rare

6. Wrong Column

Which word below is in the wrong column?

head	bear
view	dogs
boil	foot
haul	pins
land	mine

7. Odd One Out

Which set of arrows is the odd one out?

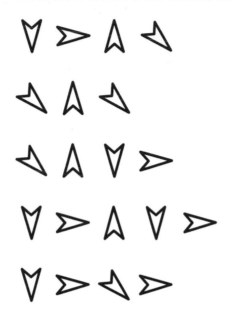

8. Missing Word

joker

reach

towel

lodge

Which word below is missing from the above list, and where should it be placed?

final, habit, horse, chart, index?

9. Pair Up

Find a reason for arranging these ten words into five groups of two words each.

vision	access	column	Indian	plated
random	spinal	summer	tunnel	armour

10. Two Columns

locate	basket
unmown	poetic
debtor	ravage
	creche
	?

What word below should replace the question mark?

policy, length, square, people, height

X - Miscellaneous

1. Fruit Squash

Place one of the fruits in the first column between one of the groups of letters in the second column until you have produced six words.

For example: GRD + APPLE = GRAPPLED

date	subly
peach	aped
lime	bng
pear	sed
ugli	efy
fig	imment

2. Rebuses

A rebus is the enigmatic representation in visual form of the sounds of a name or word. Rebus is a Latin word meaning *by things*, indicating a coded text which can be deciphered by studying its visual display.

The solving of rebuses often call for a degree of lateral, or creative, thinking. The types of rebuses which follow became popular during the 1970s and more recently have become popular in newspapers and magazines. The solution may be a phrase, or just one word, and two examples are as follows:

a)

Never a cross word

N   N

     E   E

          V

     E   E

R   R

b)

The Andes

T H E
&
EEEEEEEE

Now try to solve the following:

I.	II.	III.
U N T A O I M N	N W O D	A M P T G I S G N
IV.	V.	VI.
OH FEART	• ERV •	
VII.	VIII.	IX.
	POINT	O2H
X.	XI.	XII.
	THE 12" DOOR	RLIGL

3. T - Words

Always using the **central letter T** find as many words as possible of four letters or more. Letters cannot be repeated in any particular word, but need not be next to each other in the grid. There is one 9 - letter word.

P   U   R

A   **T**   H

I   L   M

Examples of 4 - letters words: trim, path

4. Mouse - Hole

Change **MOUSE** to **HOLE** by producing compound words at each stage with the aid of the letters provided, for example: change BLACK to HOLE by proceeding black - mail - man - hole.

M O U S E

* * A *

* O * R

* T * *

* A * H * *

* * N *

* A * K

* * M *

* U *

* O *

H O L E

5. Odd One Out

Which word is the odd one out?

intoxicate	senator	madden	regiment	reaction
demand	observe	excitation	teach	creation
statement	verbose	treason	cheat	testament

6. Network

Move from letter to connected letter to spell out a 14 - letter word.
Every letter must be used once each only.

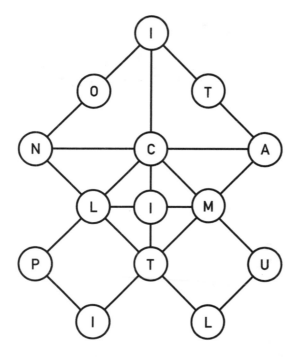

Namystics first appeared in the 1920s. They can be played with your own name, place names, famous people, words or phrases.

All you need is a blank outline thus:

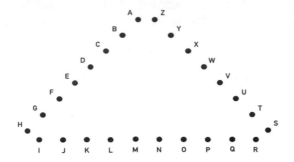

Starting with the first letter of the chosen name draw a straight line to the second letter, then to the third and so on. Double-letters are treated as if they were a single letter.

For example:

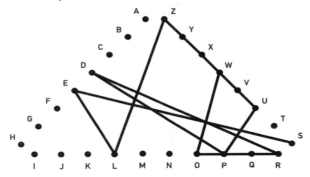

Answer: word puzzles

Now try to solve the following which are either names, phrases or just one word as indicated:

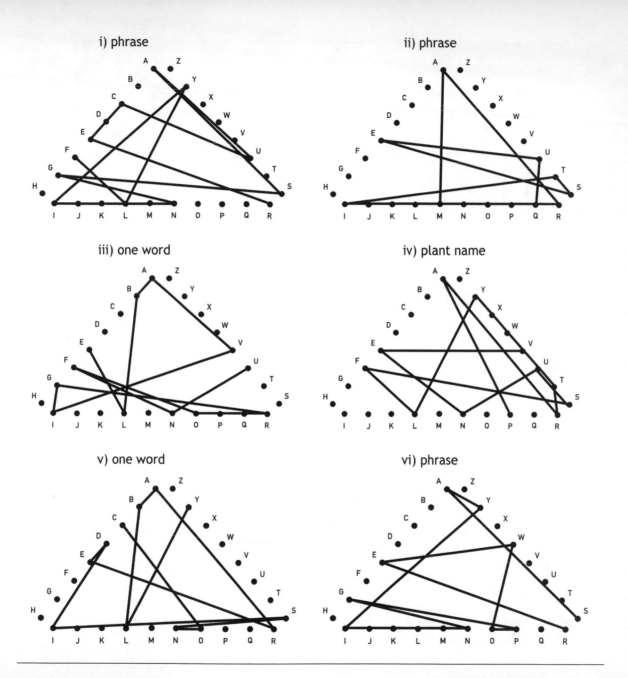

i) phrase

ii) phrase

iii) one word

iv) plant name

v) one word

vi) phrase

8. Quarter The Square

Divide the square into four segments of equal size and shape. Each segment must contain the same nine letters which can be arranged into a 9 - letter word.

M	S	C	C	N	S
O	T	N	I	T	L
S	U	L	O	M	O
O	U	I	U	M	U
M	C	I	I	T	S
T	N	L	L	N	C

9. Knight's Move

Using the Knight's move in chess:

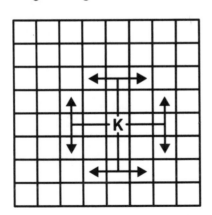

D			C	
	K	H		
	O		E	E
	C	B		
U				L

find the stating point and move from letter to letter to spell out a phrase which is both a phrase used in chess and also in general usage.

10. Fight And Play

Each of the following word combinations rhymes with a well-known phrase, for example *fight and play* rhymes with *night and day*.

Can you work out the phrases?

rock and scull	fat and log	rebut and begun
chew and fry	stun and dames	then and stink
cup and crown	feeling and ceiling	madam and relieve
cigars and pipes	sigh and charge	flat and dowse

11. Odds And Ends

Each three-word phrase has been hidden by removing the initial letters of each word and then removing the space between them.

For example *odds and ends* would become DDSNDNDS and *get the message* would become ETHEESSAGE

ATUMBLEIE	ONEHEISER	AKEOEART
ARNDEACE	TONGAST	NOODHAPE
ALLNTOLACE	OREATHAKES	EVENEARTCH

12. Trackword

Find a 10-letter word by travelling from circle to adjoining circle in any direction.

The puzzle itself provides a clue to the answer.

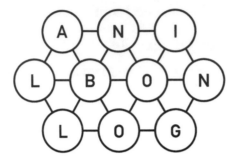

13. Saying

All the vowels have been removed from this trite saying and the remaining consonants split into four groups of eight. What is the saying? All the consonants remain in the same order.

THDFFCLT   **SSYNDTHM**   **PSSBLSLT**   **TLBTHRDR**

14. Doublets

Invented in 1879 by Lewis Carroll, the puzzle which he named *Doublets* but which is now probably better known as *Word Ladders*, consists of proposing two words of the same length and converting one word into the other by changing one letter at a time and forming new words at each stage. The new words formed are called links, for example change HEAD into TAIL in four links: solution HEAD - HEAL - TEAL - TELL - TALL - TAIL; heal, teal, tell and tall being the four links.

Now try the following:

i) Change **PIG** to **STY** in 4 links

ii) Change **HAND** to **FOOT** in 5 links

iii) Change **MORE** to **LESS** in 3 links

15. Hidden Trees

i) Find three trees hidden in the following two sentences:

I strode out quickly over the firm ground

The clothes were soaking in the wash tub

ii) Find a tree in each of the following sentences

Grandmother always used to boil the tea kettle whenever we went to visit

The battalion was ordered to slope arms prior to inspection

Named for the Roman god of war, Mars is also sometimes referred to as the red planet

Answers

I - Warm Ups

1. Verbosity

Throwing a spanner in the works

2. Find A Phrase

Out of circulation

3. Animals

Reindeer, nyala, opossum, gorilla, koala, onager, antelope, armadillo

Anagram: **kangaroo**

4. Letter Change

odd one out

call the tune

in deep water

other fish to fry

a miss is as good as a mile

on the boil

cut and dried

keep an eye out

lay down the law

pass the buck

5. Saying In Bits

Look a gift horse in the mouth

6. Add a Letter

All sea going vessels - dhow, raft, sloop, brig, punt, barge, canoe

7. Geezer's Teasers

wide stride	slyer friar
scare Blair	dream team
lacking backing	scan plan
brain drain	grip whip
Llama drama	ration passion

8. Two Sayings

too many cooks spoil the broth

many hands make light work (mark my shaking hand-towel)

9. Find The Word

Wind

10. Missing Link

End

11. XYZ

XYZ = law

lawyer, clawed, Malawi, outlaw

12. Code Word

MINERAL	(ENIGMA)	KINGDOM
ASTAIRE	(ANSWER)	TINWARE
3 1 6	1 2 3 4 5 6	2 4 5

13. Bracket Link Word

tape/pert, side/desk, most/star, meal/ally

8 - letter word : pedestal

14. Three - Letter Words

Madeleine : to give hum, sea, nod, foe, owl, toe, ski, ran, cue

15. Find A Word

acronym

second b<u>a</u>llot

centre of Chi<u>c</u>ago

sixth forme<u>r</u>

first <u>o</u>ffender

<u>n</u>on-starter

satisfactor<u>y</u> conclusion

botto<u>m</u> end

16. Tiles

E R T|O O	B U|P B	M U O

N
S W|E
I
	E
	  M|E
	G
		F
		  N
		A

S
E N|O
R
	O
	  O|R
	I
		T
		  L
		A

the two related words which appear around the outer edge are *serial number*

17. No Vowels

For better or for worse

---

18. Palindromes

A

Niagara, O **roar** again

Dennis and **Edna** sinned

Now Ned I am a **maiden** nun, Ned I am a maiden won

Snug & raw was I ere **I saw** war & guns

Sums are not set as a test on **Erasmus**

Nurse, I spy **gypsies** run

Sir, I demand, I am a **maid** named Iris

Kay, a red nude **peeped** under a yak

Doc, note, I dissent, a fast never prevents a **fatness** I diet on cod.

'Tis **Ivan** on a visit

B

A dog! A panic in a pagoda

19. Pangram

The five boxing wizards jump quickly

20. Complete The Crossword

Starling: the theme is birds

21. Perimeter Words

melodrama, testimony, geometric

22. Non-Stop

perpetual motion

23. Antonyms

hop	dead	-	**hope**	**dread**
boar	lad	-	**board**	**land**
solid	right	-	**stolid**	**bright**
reel	raw	-	**repel**	**draw**
beak	coy	-	**bleak**	**cosy**

24. Conversions

A	B
ICE	ROD
ACE	ROT
ATE	POT
SKATER	PIT
	PISTON

25. Word Circle

secure, rebuke, kennel, elapse

II - Anagrams

1. Anagram Theme

The theme is musical instruments:- clarinet - ant relic, trombone - robot men, accordion - acid croon

2. Managra

hysterical

3. Enigmagram

trimaran, schooner, lifeboat, waterbus
Key anagram: **submarine**

4. Vegetables

drain man = mandarin

The vegetables are:
cash pin - **spinach**
take choir - **artichoke**
spin rap - **parsnip**
cult tee - **lettuce**
war secrets - **watercress**

5. Find the Word

LORMTA = mortal

6. Six Anagrams

post, stop, spot, tops, pots, opts

7. Ouch !

bed of nails

8. Anagrammed Synonyms

penitent - sorry

similar - alike

enthusiast - fan

detailed - exact

proficient - able

erstwhile - late

9. Liberate Tennis

i) imagination, ii) incomprehensibility, iii) gravitation, iv) persistent, v) mysterious

10. Phrases

i) leading man, ii) sleep tight, iii) odd one out, iv) not a hope

---

11. Cryptagrams

i) graceful (Gulf race), ii) bibliographer (glib hair probe), iii) righteousness (resting houses), iv) transship (spin trash)

12. Antonyms

plausible, illogical

13. Synonyms

equipment, apparatus

14. Same Sound

i. great ape   grey tape

ii. known ocean   no notion

15. Satin Stain

rapier   repair

16. Palindromic Anagrams

senile felines, name no one man, never odd or even

17. Tiny Crossword Anagram

R	A	R	E
A	R	E	A
M	I	S	S
P	A	T	E

18. BRRRRRRRRRR

north polar

19. Longest Word

upholder

20. When You Wish

shooting star

21. Numbers

fifteen, thirty five, seventy, eighty one, ninety three, three hundred, eight thousand, forty million

22. Book Titles

indisposed, sustenance, apostate, gourmet, stereotype, espionage, garrulous

23. Three Of A Kind

emerald, ruby, topaz

grape, apple, pear

horse, elephant, lion

24. Countries

saw nothing = Washington

The countries are:

and ionise = **Indonesia**

lizard newts = **Switzerland**

big Laura = **Bulgaria**

regain tan = **Argentina**

25. Animals

Tasmanian possum, European bison, bactrian camel, Pyrenean mountain dog, horseshoe bat, Patagonian cavy, sealyham terrier, Christmas beetle

26. Footprint

Friday, island, Selkirk, maroon

The link is Robinson Crusoe (Alexander Selkirk was the real-life mariner on whose life Robinson Crusoe was based)

27. Complete The Grid

28. Famous Name Anagrams

a. Barbra Streisand
b. Ferdinand Magellan
c. Andre Agassi
d. Amelia Earhart
e. Konrad Adenauer
f. Enrico Caruso
g. George Armstrong Custer
h. Rafael Sabatini
i. Benjamin Franklin
j. Sadie Thompson

29. Anagram Crossword

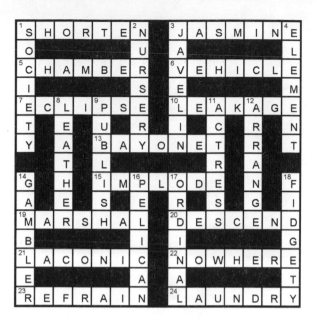

The crossword grid contains the following answers:

Across:
1. SHORTEN
3. JASMINE
5. CHAMBER
6. VEHICLE
7. ECLIPSE
10. LEAKAGE
13. BAYONET
15. IMPLODE
19. MARSHAL
20. DESCEND
21. LACONIC
22. NOWHERE
23. REFRAIN
24. LAUNDRY

Down:
1. SOCIETY
2. NURSE
4. ELEMENT
8. LEATHER
9. PURRING
11. ARRANGE
12. ARROGANT
14. GAMBLE
16. LISERA
17. ORSIGNS
18. FIGHT

30. The Good, The Bad And The Ugly

answer	anagram	synonym	antonym
continued	unnoticed	resumed	ended
glisten	singlet	shimmer	fade
considerate	desecration	thoughtful	negligent
resign	singer	quit	enlist
nadir	drain	base	top
fluster	restful	agitate	placate
education	cautioned	learning	illiteracy
lament	mental	bewail	rejoice
dearth	thread	insufficiency	abundance

III - Crosswords

1. Word-Cross Puzzle

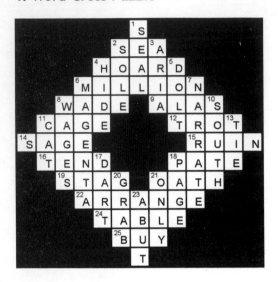

2. 9 x 9 Crossword

3. 12 x 12 Crossword I

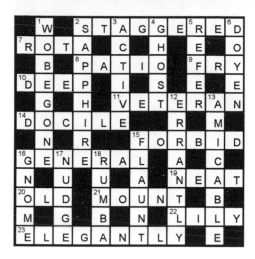

4. 12 x 12 Crossword II

5. 15 x 15 Crossword

6. The MI5 And Mr Dawe

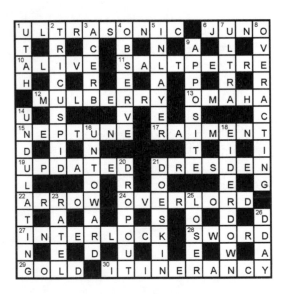

7. 12 x 12 Barred

A	B	O	R	I	G	I	N	A	L	S	S
R	E	P	E	N	T	M	O	R	A	T	E
A	L	E	I	S	O	P	T	I	C	A	L
S	O	N	N	E	T	O	E	S	U	R	F
S	W	I	M	R	N	S	T	E	W	E	D
E	I	N	S	T	E	I	N	N	S	R	E
S	D	G	P	A	G	N	O	S	T	I	C
S	I	E	R	R	A	G	R	J	O	K	E
M	A	K	E	F	T	R	I	M	I	N	I
E	P	S	T	E	I	N	G	E	C	E	T
N	E	P	A	L	V	K	I	G	A	L	I
T	R	E	X	T	E	R	N	A	L	L	Y

8. Cryptic Crossword I

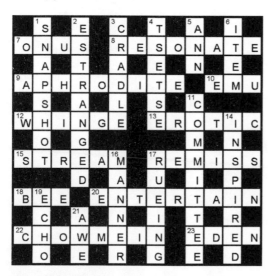

9. Cryptic Crossword II

10. Cryptic Crossword III

11. Cryptic Crossword IV

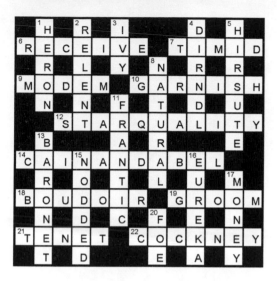

IV - Crosswords Variations

1. X-Word Search

2. Crossjig

3. Cross crossword

4. 7 x 7 Consonant Mix

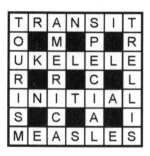

5. Words in Circulation

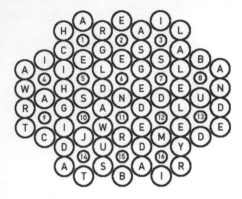

1. charge, 2. grease, 3. assail, 4. Hawaii, 5. shield, 6. legend, 7. sledge,
8. unable, 9. tragic, 10. jigsaw, 11. wander, 12. meddle, 13. eluded,
14. adjust, 15. absurd, 16. myriad

6. Alphabet Crossword

7. Daffynitions

		a guard singing Bach	centrifugal
		a bomb in a parrot	politics
		Asian jewellery	orienteering
		a hooker's fee	tartrate
		how the cannibal felt about his mother-in-law	gladiator
		an advocate of SI units	programme
		what one should be in genteel company	extrapolate
		a devilish stretch of water	demonstrate
		a USA campaign slogan in the 1980s	electron
		keep the door ajar	propagate

a guard singing Bach — centrifugal
a bomb in a parrot — politics
Asian jewellery — orienteering
a hooker's fee — tartrate
how the cannibal felt about his mother-in-law — gladiator
an advocate of SI units — programme
what one should be in genteel company — extrapolate
a devilish stretch of water — demonstrate
a USA campaign slogan in the 1980s — electron
keep the door ajar — propagate

8. Missing Consonants

9. Fivers

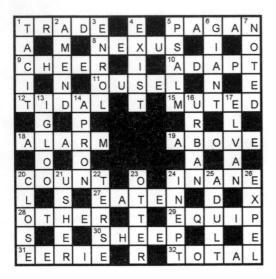

10. Cross-Alphabet

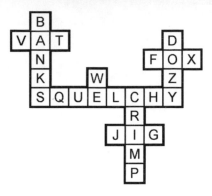

V - Acrostics

1.

	a	b	c	d	e	f	g	h	i
1	T	H	E		O	N	L	Y	
2	G	O	O	D		I	S		
3	K	N	O	W	L	E	D	G	E
4	A	N	D		T	H	E		
5	O	N	L	Y		E	V	I	L
6	I	S							
7	I	G	N	O	R	A	N	C	E

i.   Show
ii.   Oddity
iii. Challenging
iv.   Revoked
v.   Alone
vi.   Tiny
vii. Engine
viii. Solo

Socrates

2.

	a	b	c	d	e	f	g	h	i	j	k
1	T	H	E		B	I	G	G	E	S	T
2	R	E	W	A	R	D		F	O	R	
3	A		T	H	I	N	G				
4	W	E	L	L		D	O	N	E		
5	I	S		T	O		H	A	V	E	
6	D	O	N	E			I	T			

---

i. Vegetable
ii. Own
iii. Light
iv. Tight
v. Ado
vi. Isherwood
vii. Refit
viii. Ensnared

Voltaire

3.

	a	b	c	d	e	f	g	h	i	j	k	l
1	A		D	O	O	R		I	S			
2	W	H	A	T		A		D	O	G		
3	I	S										
4	P	E	R	P	E	T	U	A	L	L	Y	
5	O	N		T	H	E		W	R	O	N	G
6	S	I	D	E		O	F					

i. Owed
ii. Goof
iii. Diary
iv. Era
v. Newspaper
vi. Night
vii. Adult
viii. Solo
ix. Hoist

Ogden Nash

4.

	a	b	c	d	e	f	g	h	i	j	k	l
1	H	E			W	H	O		D	O	E	S
2	N	O	T		P	R	E	V	E	N	T	
3	A		C	R	I	M	E		W	H	E	N
4	H	E		C	A	N						
5	E	N	C	O	U	R	A	G	E	S		
6	I	T										

i. Show
ii. Entrench
iii. Nowhere
iv. Education
v. Comprehensive
vi. Agate

Seneca

5.

	a	b	c	d	e	f	g	h	i	j	k	l	m
1	T	H	E		I	M	P	O	R	T	A	N	T
2	T	H	I	N	G		I	S		N	O	T	
3	T	O		S	T	O	P						
4	Q	U	E	S	T	I	O	N	I	N	G		

i.   Equation
ii. Inns
iii. Not
iv. Spot
v.   Tight
vi. Egotist
vii. Imp
viii.North

Einstein

VI - Codes And Cryptograms

1.

Experience is a great advantage. The problem is that when you get the experience you are too old to do anything about it.

Jimmy Connors

2.

A man is a success if he gets up in the morning and gets to bed at night, and in between he does what he wants to do.

Bob Dylan

3.

Committee - a group of people who individually can do nothing but as a group decide that nothing can be done.

Fred Allen

4.

Half our life is spent trying to find something to do with the time we have rushed through life trying to save.

Will Rogers

5.

Don't worry about the world coming to an end today. It's already tomorrow in Australia.

Charles Schultz

6.

History is the version of past events that people have decided to agree upon.

Napoleon Bonaparte

7.

Nothing is as easy as it looks. Everything takes longer than you expect. If anything can go wrong, it will do so; and always at the worst possible moment.

Murphy's Law

Message keyed: **(PRESONGADL) - Press on regardless**

8. Cryptophone

i. Niagara Falls
ii. fast and furious
iii. poetry in motion
iv. comprehensible
v. laughing jackass
vi. Spanish Civil War
vii. cantilever bridge
viii. thanks for nothing

ix. black forest gateau
x. technical knockout
xi. lean over backwards
xii. foregone conclusion
xiii. once bitten twice shy
iv. Bonnie Prince Charlie
v. House of Representatives

9. Strange Notice

Keep off the grass — Read the message backwards, ignoring spacing.

10. Disney's World

If you can dream it, you can do it — All the vowels have been replaced by the letter V.

11. The Hidden Message

See me at two Sunday

At a loo**se e**nd
Ro**me**o
Ka**te**
For**t Wo**rth
goe**s un**der

12. Ale in Cans Code

To change and to improve are two different things

13. Numbergram
Truth is more of a stranger than fiction.

Mark Twain

14. The Polybius Cipher

Time's fun when you're having flies.

Kermit the Frog

According to the grid, letters are represented by their respective numbered line, followed by their numbered column i.e. the letter **T** is represented by the number 45 because it is in line **4** and column **5** as illustrated below.

	1	2	3	4	5
1	A	B	C	D	E
2	F	G	H	I	J
3	K	L	M	N	O
4	P	Q	R	S	T
5	U	V	W	X	Y

15. ID Numbers

131871820 — Ignore vowels in the names and allocate numbers to the consonants according to their position in the English alphabet.

VII - Word Search

1. What The Dickens!

```
M E A C H R I S T M A S E
U L G O F D U M U G N E D
T T W P Z O B W T O D I W
U T K P M R L Y I Y J T I
A A P E R R E T W B S I N
L B P R P I A I E A E C O
M N K F I T K S L N M H L
D X G I C E I O Z R I I H
O V H E K K H I Z A T M P
M T P L W C P R U B W E M
B X B D I I M U H I I S F
E W G N C R L C C N S H C
Y F A R K C O L C S T X C
```

Barnaby Rudge

Bleak House

A Christmas Carol

Cricket on the Hearth

David Copperfield

Domby and Son

Edwin Drood

Great Expectations

Hard Times

Little Dorrit

Martin Chuzzlewit

Master Humphrey's Clock

The Mudfog Papers

Nicholas Nickleby

The Old Curiosity Shop

Oliver Twist

Our Mutual Friend

Pickwick Papers

Sketches by Boz

A Tale of Two Cities

The Battle of Life

The Chimes

2. Trivia Search

R	S	Y	M	B	I	R	D	P	N
E	T	A	L	E	L	R	N	R	O
N	A	T	I	L	O	P	A	E	N
A	G	S	E	B	H	O	L	W	A
Z	E	I	G	A	E	L	E	T	G
Z	C	L	E	T	N	I	C	N	O
I	O	K	M	S	G	S	A	A	N
P	A	V	O	N	R	H	R	X	A
I	C	C	R	O	I	V	G	O	I
L	H	U	A	C	N	X	U	N	P

i. Lohengrin

ii. nonagon

iii. Lipizzaner

iv. Tay

v. Constable

vi. Polish

vii. Graceland

viii. bird

ix. Antwerp Liege

x. silk

xi. Neapolitan

xii. Rome

xiii. piano

xiv. Stagecoach

3. United States Presidents

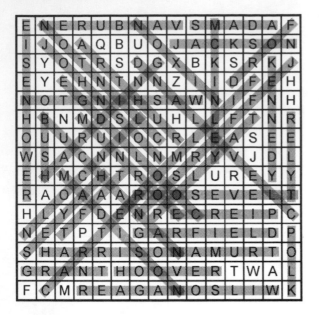

```
E N E R U B N A V S M A D A F
I J O A Q B U O J A C K S O N
S Y O T R S D G X B K S R K J
E Y E H N T N N Z I I D F E H
N O T G N I H S A W N I F N H
H B N M D S L U H L L F T N R
O U U R U I O C R L E A S E E
W S A C N N L N M R Y V J D L
E H M C H T R O S L U R E Y Y
R A O A A A R O O S E V E L T
H L Y F D E N R E C R E I P C
N E T P T I G A R F I E L D P
S H A R R I S O N A M U R T O
G R A N T H O O V E R T W A L
F C M R E A G A N O S L I W K
```

Adams, Arthur, Buchanan, Bush, Carter, Cleveland, Clinton, Coolidge, Eisenhower, Fillmore, Ford, Garfield, Grant, Harding, Harrison, Hayes, Hoover, Jackson, Jefferson, Johnson, Kennedy, Lincoln, Madison, McKinley, Munroe, Nixon, Pierce, Polk, Reagan, Roosevelt, Taft, Taylor, Truman, Tyler, VanBuran, Washington, Wilson

4. Half A Phrase

```
I  B  A  L  L  P  O  I  N  T  I  Q  W  V  T
N  O  I  T  A  I  C  O  S  S  A  W  P  V  H
H  I  P  P  O  C  R  A  T  I  C  A  P  O  G
E  T  A  T  E  D  Y  T  O  N  L  K  F  B  I
R  N  T  I  S  I  E  E  D  I  B  E  E  Y  L
I  E  H  T  S  R  L  L  M  V  B  L  M  K  Y
T  M  E  N  O  E  G  E  M  U  L  E  V  X  A
A  E  T  A  R  C  N  P  I  A  K  V  D  D  D
N  S  I  H  C  T  U  H  D  H  T  E  N  I  V
C  A  C  C  A  I  J  O  S  C  S  N  O  S  A
E  B  S  R  L  O  N  N  U  I  P  T  I  A  N
Z  M  Y  E  H  N  X  E  M  N  P  H  T  S  T
J  V  N  M  A  U  T  O  M  A  T  I  C  T  A
D  T  H  C  A  O  R  P  E  R  Z  N  A  E  G
O  X  W  P  U  P  V  T  R  E  A  S  U  R  E
```

action replay

vantage point

above reproach

disaster movie

stage direction

male chauvinist

daylight robbery

word association

pathetic fallacy

promised land

wine merchant

lacrosse stick

concrete jungle

automatic pilot

belladonna lily

press conference

bargain basement

eleventh hour

ballpoint pen

treasure trove

midsummer night

inheritance tax

alimentary canal

telephone number

hippocratic oath

5. Countries

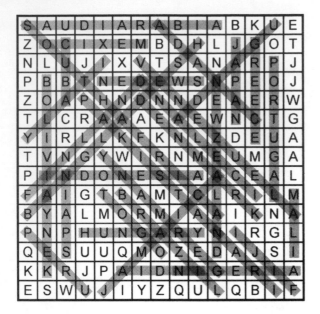

S	A	U	D	I	A	R	A	B	I	A	B	K	U	E
Z	O	C	I	X	E	M	B	D	H	L	J	G	O	T
N	L	U	J	I	X	V	T	S	A	N	A	R	P	J
P	B	B	T	N	E	D	E	W	S	N	P	E	O	J
Z	O	A	P	H	N	D	N	N	D	E	A	E	R	W
T	L	C	R	A	A	A	E	A	E	W	N	C	T	G
Y	I	R	L	L	K	F	K	N	L	Z	D	E	U	A
T	V	N	G	Y	W	I	R	N	M	E	U	M	G	A
P	I	N	D	O	N	E	S	I	A	A	C	E	A	L
F	A	I	G	T	B	A	M	T	C	L	R	I	L	M
B	Y	A	L	M	O	R	M	A	A	I	K	N	A
P	N	P	H	U	N	G	A	R	Y	N	I	R	G	L
Q	E	S	U	U	Q	M	O	Z	E	D	A	J	S	I
K	K	R	J	P	A	I	D	N	I	G	E	R	I	A
E	S	W	U	J	I	Y	Z	Q	U	L	Q	B	I	F

Bangladesh, Bolivia, Brazil, Canada, Cuba, Denmark, Fiji, Finland, Germany, Greece, Hungary, Iceland, India, Indonesia, Iran, Italy, Jamaica, Japan, Kenya, Mali, Mexico, New Zealand, Nigeria, Pakistan, Peru, Portugal, Saudi Arabia, South Africa, Spain, Sri Lanka, Sweden, Togo, Uganda, Venezuela

VIII - Magic Word Squares

1. Blended Magic

```
R A N           P E A
A G O           E E L
N O W A S P       A R E A L L
    A X E L       R E A P
    S E R E       E A S E
    P L E A R E N A P E X
        R A D I I
        E D G E D
        N I E C E
    S A G A I D E D A M P
    A C E R       A R I A
    G E R M       M I L L
S E A R M Y       P A L M E W
E R R             E G O
A R T             W O N
```

2. 5 x 5 Numbered

¹S	²H	³R	⁴E	⁵D
⁶H	E	A	V	E
⁷R	A	B	A	T
⁸E	V	A	D	E
⁹D	E	T	E	R

3. 4 x 4 Anagram

R	O	A	R
O	N	C	E
A	C	M	E
R	E	E	F

4. 5 x 5 Blended Numbered

¹E	²N	³A	⁴C	⁵T
⁶N	O	B	L	E
⁷A	B	E	A	M
⁸C	L	A	M	P
⁹T	E	M	P	T

¹⁰R	¹¹E	¹²S	¹³S	
¹⁴R	A	N	C	H
¹⁵E	N	S	U	E
¹⁶S	C	U	B	A
¹⁷S	H	E	A	R

5. 5 x 5 Consonants

P	L	A	C	E
L	E	G	A	L
A	G	O	R	A
C	A	R	A	T
E	L	A	T	E

6. 5 x 5 Unnumbered

S	M	A	S	H
M	A	N	I	A
A	N	G	E	R
S	I	E	G	E
H	A	R	E	M

7. 5 x 5 Anagram

S	M	A	S	H
M	A	N	I	A
A	N	G	E	R
S	I	E	G	E
H	A	R	E	M

8. 6 x 6 Unnumbered

R	A	S	C	A	L
A	C	T	I	V	E
S	T	A	T	E	D
C	I	T	I	N	G
A	V	E	N	G	E
L	E	D	G	E	R

9. 4 x 4 Blended Unnumbered

10. Blended Unnumbered

L	A	M	P				A	L	A	S
A	B	E	L				L	A	N	E
M	E	N	U				A	N	E	W
P	L	U	S	T	R	E	S	S	E	W	N
			T	R	E	N	C	H		
			R	E	C	T	O	R		
			E	N	T	I	R	E		
			S	C	O	R	E	D		
H	I	S	S	H	R	E	D	S	W	A	N
I	O	T	A				W	I	P	E
S	T	E	M				A	P	E	X
S	A	M	E				N	E	X	T

IX - Lateral Thinking

1. Addition

ninety — each word carries a number in reverse:

d**eno**te + e**xis**tence + bl**owt**orch = awak**ening**
sol**eno**id + indig**eno**us = k**owt**ow
undergr**owt**h + regr**owt**h + Mar**xis**ts = ni**net**y

2. Find the Sequence

cloud — the vowels appear in repeated sequence: a, e, i, o, u

3. Find the Lady

Agatha — the sequence of letters a, b, c, d, e, f, g, h
appear in the same position in each of the words.

4. Something in common

They all have a mountainous link:

lem(ur	al)cove	Ural
sc(alp	s)nake	Alps
c(rock	y)ield	Rocky
st(and	es)py	Andes

---

5. Pairs

Pair them so that each of the 4 - letter words is an anagram of the last four letters of one of the names in List A:

Belgrade - dear
Canberra - rare
Alicante - neat
Labrador - road
Dordogne - gone
Pamplona - loan
Barbados - soda

6. Wrong Column

bear — all words in the first column can be prefixed with *over*.
All the words in the second column can be prefixed with *under*.

7. Odd One Out

The bottom set, as all the others
spell S - E - N - S - E
as illustrated below:

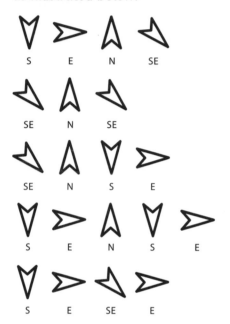

8. Missing Word

habit — so that all words start with
the last letter of the preceding word:

joker, reach, *habit*, towel, lodge

9. Pair Up

random - access
Indian - summer
armour - plated
spinal - column
tunnel - vision

10. Two Columns

length — the numbers ONE and TWO are
spelled down the first three words.
The numbers SEVEN and EIGHT are spelled
down the second five words.

```
LO CATE        BASKET
UNMOWN         POETIC
DE B TOR       RAVAGE
               CRECHE
               LENGTH
```

X - Miscellaneous

1. Fruit Squash

sedated, effigy, sublimely, appeared, impeachment, bugling

2. Rebuses

i) **Table Mountain** (the word mountain in the shape of a table)
ii) **upside-down** (the word *down* written up the side of the box)
iii) **stamping ground** (the word stamping round the letter G)
iv) **change of heart** (the F and H from *of heart* changed round)
v) **nerve centre** (ERV is the centre of the word nerve)
vi) **command** (the letters ND constructed from commas)
vii) **spring lamb**
viii) **breaking point**
ix) **backwater** (the symbol for water - H_2O - appears backwards)
x) **Mexican wave**
xi) **a foot in the door** (the symbol for foot separates *the* and *door*)
xii) **mixed grill** (the word grill has been mixed up).

3. T - words

armpit, halt, hurt, impart, part, path, ritual, tail, thump, trail, trap, trial, trip, ultra, hart, malt, mirth, pith, tapir, tram, tramp, trim, trump, tulip, hilt, lath, mart, multi, plait, rapt, Tamil, thrum, atrium, ruth, triumph.
9- letter word: **triumphal**

---

4. Mouse - Hole

M O U S E
T R A P
D O O R
S T E P
F A T H E R
L A N D
M A R K
T I M E
O U T
F O X
H O L E

5. Odd One Out

regiment — The rest are anagram pairs: intoxicate/excitation, cheat/teach, creation/reaction, statement/testament, senator/treason, observe/verbose, demand/madden

6. Network

multiplication

7. Namystics

i) flying saucer
ii) question mark
iii) unforgivable
iv) Venus flytrap
v) considerably
vi) staying power

8. Quarter The Square

columnist

M	S	C	C	N	S
O	T	N	I	T	L
S	U	L	O	M	O
O	U	I	U	M	U
M	C	I	I	T	S
T	N	L	L	N	C

9. Knight's Move

double-check

1^D			10^C	
	11^K	8^H		
	2^O		6^E	9^E
	7^C	4^B		
3^U				5^L

10. Fight And Play

cock and bull	cat and dog	cut and run
hue and cry	fun and games	pen and ink
up and down	wheeling and dealing	Adam and Eve
stars and stripes	by and large	cat and mouse

11. Odds And Ends

eat humble pie	none the wiser	take to heart
war and peace	at long last	in good shape
fall into place	no great shakes	seven year itch

12. Trackword

ballooning

13. Saying

The difficult is easy and the impossible is a little bit harder

14. Doublets

i) PIG, **WIG, WAG, WAY, SAY**, STY
ii) HAND, **HARD, LARD, LORD, FORD, FORT**, FOOT
iii) MORE, **LORE, LOSE, LOSS**, LESS

---

15. Hidden Trees

i) fir, oak, ash
I strode out quickly over the **fir**m ground

The clothes were s**oak**ing in the w**ash** tub

ii) teak, pear, plane
Grandmother always used to boil the **tea k**ettle whenever
we went to visit

The battalion was ordered to slo**pe ar**ms prior to inspection

Named for the Roman god of war, Mars is also sometimes
referred to as the red **plane**t

puzzle books from D&B publishing

The Times – Two Brains
by Ray Keene & Byron Jacobs
1-904468-05-5, 158pp, £5.99 / $9.95

How to Solve IQ Puzzles
by Philip Carter and Ken Russell
1-904468-10-1, 174pp, £5.99 / $9.95

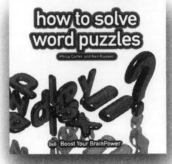

How to Solve Word Puzzles
by Philip Carter and Ken Russell
1-904468-19-5, 168pp, £5.99 / $9.95

200 Word Puzzles
by Philip Carter and Ken Russell
1-904468-03-9, 160pp, £5.99 / $9.95

400 IQ Puzzles
by Philip Carter and Ken Russell
1-904468-02-0, 174pp, £5.99 / $9.95

500 IQ Puzzles
by Philip Carter
1-904468-22-5, 176pp, £5.99 / $9.95

D&B PUBLISHING
www.dandbpublishing.com